Now What?

The day you receive a diploma is not the end.

It is the beginning!

DISCLAIMER

This book contains the opinions and ideas of its author. It is sold with the understanding that neither the author nor the publisher is engaged in rendering investment, financial, accounting, legal, tax, insurance, or other professional advice or services. If you require such advice or services, a competent professional should be consulted. The strategies outlined in this book may not be suitable for every person and are not guaranteed to produce any particular result.

No warrant is made with respect to the accuracy or completeness of the information contained herein. Both the author and publisher specifically disclaim any responsibility for any liability, loss, or risk, personal and otherwise, which is incurred as a consequence, directly or indirectly, of the use and application of any of the contents of this book.

Here is the same speech put in a way you can actually understand. I am trying to educate you, not "sell" you. No one is paying me to hype his or her products. This book is designed to educate you so you can make good decisions with your money and avoid the bad ones.

No individual situation is the same. One way does not work for everyone. I realize many people struggle to just survive in this world. You may find yourself in a situation where you have few options. I encourage you to find ways to apply what you read in this book as best you can. Education can help when life seems hopeless.

Find ways around the obstacles in your life. The power lies within you and your ability to change the way you think and act. Never forget that, and never give up. You truly do have the ability to change the course of your life. Believe that, and believe in yourself.

This book is dedicated to the United States Army and the men and women who make it great. Thank you.

CONTENTS

Now What?

Foreword

Introduction

LIFE AFTER GRADUATION

Chapter 1   What Are You Going to Do?

Chapter 2   Time to Grow Up

Chapter 3   Time to Grow Down

Chapter 4   Is Life Fair?

Chapter 5   Lost and Confused

Chapter 6   Forever the Student

Chapter 7   Take a Break

Chapter 8   Opening and Closing Doors

Chapter 9   Work is a Good Thing

Chapter 10   Success?

Chapter 11   The Stories We Tell

Chapter 12   Education vs. Knowledge

Chapter 13	No College?
Chapter 14	Learn and Earn
Chapter 15	The Military
Chapter 16	The Parents
Chapter 17	The Leader
Chapter 18	The President
Chapter 19	The Significant Other
Chapter 20	Physically and Mentally Present
Chapter 21	External vs. Internal
Chapter 22	Fame and Awards
Chapter 23	Travel
Chapter 24	The Keystone Habit
Chapter 25	Dear Michael

FINANCES AFTER GRADUATION

Chapter 26	Financial Freedom
Chapter 27	Getting Started
Chapter 28	The First Big Job

Chapter 29	Monthly Payments
Chapter 30	Stuff
Chapter 31	Big Ticket Purchases
Chapter 32	The 50/50 Rule
Chapter 33	Retirement Plans
Chapter 34	The Roth IRA
Chapter 35	Spending Part I
Chapter 36	Spending Part II
Chapter 37	Spending Part III
Chapter 38	Credit Part I
Chapter 39	Credit Part II
Chapter 40	Credit Part III
Chapter 41	Debt Part I
Chapter 42	Debt Part II
Chapter 43	Debt Part III
Chapter 44	Student Loans Part I
Chapter 45	Student Loans Part II
Chapter 46	Student Loans Part III
Chapter 47	Saving Part I

Chapter 48	Saving Part II
Chapter 49	Saving Part III
Chapter 50	Investing Part I
Chapter 51	Investing Part II
Chapter 52	Investing Part III
Chapter 53	The Transfer
Chapter 54	Insurance Part I
Chapter 55	Insurance Part II
Chapter 56	Insurance Part III
Chapter 57	Buying a Vehicle Part I
Chapter 58	Buying a Vehicle Part II
Chapter 59	Buying a Vehicle Part III
Chapter 60	Buying a Home Part I
Chapter 61	Buying a Home Part II
Chapter 62	Buying a Home Part III
Chapter 63	Taxes Part I
Chapter 64	Taxes Part II
Chapter 65	Taxes Part III

THE BIG PICTURE

Chapter 66   Consciousness

Chapter 67   Enough?

Chapter 68   Helping Others

Chapter 69   You are Dying

Chapter 70   The Hero

Glossary

Now What?

My name is Mike Finley, and I am known far and wide as The Crazy Man in the Pink Wig. I have written three books: _Financial Happine$$_, _What Color is the Sky_ and _Graduation!_. This book is designed to help that person who graduates from some type of system and is provided a piece of paper as proof of their accomplishments. At that point, many individuals ask themselves a very important question, "Now What?"

Now What? is a book that intends to help that high school or college graduate who is seeking the answers to life beyond that piece of paper and the pomp and circumstance that comes with it. A diploma may open more doors for you, but those doors can close quickly without the understanding of knowing what to do when entering a "new world."

The goal of this book is to help you find the truth amongst the noise that we call life. What will that diploma get you and what will it not? I will address the issue of cost when it comes to getting those certifications and whether the debt is worth what you have been told or whether you would be wise to pass on conventional wisdom and go a different direction.

Ultimately, it will be the decisions YOU make that will determine the course of YOUR life after getting that diploma. It is crucial that you make informed decisions based on the truth rather than a bunch of loosely connected ideas that may translate into a life that can lead to suffering. Strap yourself in. This could be one very bumpy ride!

"There is no end to education. It is not that you read a book, pass an examination, and finish with education. The whole of life, from the moment you are born to the moment you die, is a process of learning."

- **Jiddu Krishnamurti**

Foreword

I met Mike Finley my freshman year of college at the University of Northern Iowa. He sat next to me in a humanities lecture with over 250 other students. At first, I despised him. He always had extra questions for the professor at the end of each class, so we never got out on time.

He was obviously paying attention in the lecture and reading all the assignments that were assigned, so naturally, we would become study partners. Fin is a passionate learner, fabulous teacher, and an even better friend. It seems to me, meeting him was much more than luck.

After study sessions, we would discuss all kinds of topics. When the world of money came up I'd always have a biblical reference come to mind, but I usually tried to avoid the topic altogether. I had absolutely no idea what Fin was talking about most of the time.

I felt digging too much into the terminology would stir up greed or cause some discontentment in my heart. Fin's message does the total opposite. It opened my eyes to appreciate what was around me and take responsibility for who I was and the image I had of my future.

I started attending Fin's financial literacy classes the same year we met. I'd control the clicker and change slides while listening just enough to keep the slides rolling. *Things quickly changed.* By my second year of college I reinvested my college savings into low cost index mutual funds, moving the money away from my parent's "helper."

This feeling of empowerment came over me as I acquired the confidence to take control of my money, pushing the "smart" financial people away. Over the next four years, I started diving into the information, reading books Fin lent me here and there, and by my senior year I was even doing a little public speaking of my own. I had become the teacher!

After I grew in my financial knowledge, I began to truly appreciate the opportunity to be a steward of my money. Having a sound financial plan takes the pressure off "what I am supposed to do." Instead, it has helped me focus on what I can do to impact others. I felt empowered along the way even as I tackled the difficulties with sustaining my new habits.

During my senior year of college, I was accepted into a competitive graduate program. The program I had prayed and dreamed about for years. However, when the time came, I declined and chose an internship with a team of Fee-Only Financial Planners. I had discovered a new passion. I continue that journey today; seeing where it takes me.

Fin helped me change my life. He was there for me every step of the way, just as he can be there for you. He presents the information in such a way that it's bound to stick. I became more aware of money, time, and life as I moved away from going through the motions.

This message becomes a mindset, and the mindset can lead to action, and the action will help you achieve your goals. For generations to come the financially literate will live differently—be a part of that! Dream bigger, reach higher, and stretch farther than you ever thought possible.

Take control of your future! Fin (and me) believes in the individual and the power they possess. If we educate ourselves and take these steps together, we will have a greater impact on the world around us. Take the next right step. Read this book!

Proudly wearing my pink wig,

Amy Gingrich, College Graduate

Introduction

I have received many diploma's in my life. Some meant more to me than others. The first one that meant anything, came when I graduated from high school. I remember it like it was yesterday. I walked across the stage and some old guy in a suit smiled at me, handed me a diploma and said, "Good job." I smiled back and said thank you.

I had finally reached the end, or so I thought. I looked forward to the day when I could ditch this classroom stuff and get on with my life. Well, I got what I wanted and then I was reminded of the saying, "Be careful what you wish for, you might just get it." I looked down at that piece of paper and said, "Now What?"

Here is the truth, I was scared to death as I asked myself that simple question. Adult after adult had been asking me what I was going to do with my life after high school and I provided answers that I thought they wanted to hear. The truth? I had no clue what I wanted to do with the rest of my life and it scared the &%*# out of me!

This book is written for those individuals who are seeking those answers to life's BIG questions. I recommend you proceed one chapter at a time in the order in which the book is written. The glossary in the back of the book will provide more detailed information on some of the new financial words and concepts you see along the way. Let's get started.

"A graduation ceremony is an event where the commencement speaker tells thousands of students dressed in identical caps and gowns that individuality is the key to success."
                                - Robert Orben

LIFE

AFTER

GRADUATION

1

WHAT ARE YOU GOING TO DO?

This is the question that most high school and college graduates are asked from many well-meaning adults. It's asked so much that I think the average graduate just starts spouting off stuff out of the blue to get the adults off their back and out of the picture. I know that's what I did once upon a time. Why? Most young people have no freaking clue about what they are going to do with their life.

It is unlikely that a young adult would know what they are going to do with their life at such a young age. In many cases, they don't know what they are going to do next week, let alone the next few decades. Maybe you should flip the question around and ask the adults what they are going to do with the rest of their life? The reaction should be priceless. It is vitally important that you avoid making any bad decisions because you "have to."

Bad decisions? Doing what others tell you to do instead of what your internal compass says you should do. It is easy to live a life that others say you should live. You just kind of go along for the ride without any great thought or concern. Don't let that happen to you. You have one life. Make it a great one. How? Start looking within for the things that bring you some sense of real fulfillment. What makes you feel good about yourself?

So, what questions should the old people be asking? What do you enjoy doing? What do you think you would enjoy doing if you haven't quite found what it is you like right now? What does your dream job look like if you could pick one? What book are you reading? What person or blog are you following? There are many questions someone could ask without causing more anxiety. The graduate with the new diploma has enough problems without the adults in the room adding to them.

Here is what I would say if I was young and some adult asked me that very difficult question about my future, "I have no freaking idea and I don't expect to know any time soon." That should move the conversation forward quickly and help you avoid saying something that isn't true.

You don't have to know what you are going to do after receiving a diploma. *It will take plenty of time to figure that out.* What you end up doing for the rest of your life is very important. Be patient with the process and keep things simple for the time being. How?

Take small steps and listen to your inner voice. If you don't think you're ready for college, don't go. Go get a job and make some money as you think things through. Take some time to grow outside the classroom and that means seeking knowledge beyond your education. Knowledge?

Knowledge is picked up informally outside the classroom. It is essential for you to know this key point. Pick up a book and start reading because you want to, not because some teacher told you to. This will better prepare you for the classroom if and/or when you are ready.

We all proceed at a different pace with our life and for many people, including myself, a break from the classroom is needed to better understand ourselves and what we want to do with our lives. So, take some time to find yourself and never stop learning about life and about YOU.

"Those who improve with age embrace the power of personal growth and personal achievement and begin to replace youth with wisdom, innocence with understanding, and lack of purpose with self-actualization."

- **Bo Bennett**

2

TIME TO GROW UP

There comes a point in our lives when we realize it's time to grow up and become an adult. Some individuals handle this issue quite well, but many of us (including myself) need a swift kick in the rear at the right time by the right people to get us started with life. I would like to take you back in time about 35 years to see one example of what may be necessary for you or someone you love.

I had graduated from high school with a diploma, but I had no real education or understanding of the world that I was entering. I was adrift in this big world with no clue about what to do next. *I was terrified.* So, I did what most people do when they are scared, I played it safe in my secure and sheltered environment instead of entering the scary world "out there." I hunkered down in my safe and secure home.

A few weeks after graduation, my father gave me an ultimatum when he said, "Find another place to live before the year is out." My dad was telling me it was time to grow up. A few weeks later, I signed up for a scary place called the United States Army. Looking back in time, my father provided a bit of tough love exactly when it was necessary. It was one of the best things he ever did for me.

I stumbled a bit in finding my way. That is how it works for most of us. There are good days and there are bad days and everyone who goes through the process of growing up can relate to that experience, but here is the key point that I want to make. In many instances, we need someone in our life to give us a shove even when we don't think we are ready. If we all waited until we were ready for the world, there would be a lot of people still living with mom and dad back home.

Here is a message I needed to hear. Overcoming your fears is hard, but it is a necessary part of living a meaningful life if you hope to realize your true potential. Seeking safety and comfort will not serve you well in the long run. You cannot make life safe no matter how hard you try. Life is not safe and we all need to accept that reality as we enter the world.

Mom and dad cannot protect their children from the horrors of life no matter how hard they try. There comes a point when the parents must let go even though the future is unknown and full of pitfalls. It does require a bit of courage, hope, optimism and even a bit of luck. Parents need to let go and children need to venture out into the great unknown.

At some point, the baby bird must leave the nest no matter how warm and safe it appears to be. If the little bird stays too long, those wings may not fully develop. Fly they must. And when the baby bird falls (and that will happen at times), the baby bird needs to get up and try again. That's how baby birds learn to fly. Flight comes to those who stumble.

Sometimes the best way to show our love is to let people fail and I want you to know that failing is not the worst thing in the world. Allowing ourselves to find our way will make us stronger as we deal with the inevitable struggles that make up life. Parents need to hear that and so do the baby birds that we call graduates. It's time to fly.

"For the timid, change is frightening; for the comfortable change is threatening; but for the confident, change is opportunity."

- **Nido Qubein**

3

TIME TO GROW DOWN

There are many times in life when you and I should look in the mirror and accept our ignorance. When we are ready and willing to do that, it will be time to "grow down." It can be a humbling experience, but a positive one, if we know how to handle life and its many unknowns.

To grow down is about growing from within. It is about being honest with yourself. Some people puff their chest out and act like they know something they don't. They are playing smart as they attempt to appear wiser on a topic than they really are. This approach leaves holes in a person's education and knowledge. The better option is to play dumb.

Play dumb? To play dumb is to act as if you know little on a topic so you can learn more about it from as many sources as possible. Playing dumb is a method that allows you to receive information that the guy playing smart will not get. It does take a humble person to say I don't know, but it can make all the difference in the world.

Will some people make you feel stupid for not knowing on one subject or another? Sure they will, but so what. The kind of person who bullies you over not knowing something is not the kind of person you want in your life. They are weak and the way they show it is by harassing you. Distance yourself from those people.

To be curious about life and the people in it is at the root of this idea of growing down. The person who stays curious will seek answers where others will not. They will dig deep to understand at a deeper level and are not afraid to declare ignorance on one topic or another. Saying I don't know is to say, "I want to learn more."

So, how do you apply this concept to your everyday life? When someone is discussing something with you on a topic that you have yet to master, instead of nodding your head and saying, "I got it," keep your head still and ask questions to the "teacher" to clarify the points and add depth to what you are learning. This could lead you to specialize on that subject.

Specialize? To master a specific area of interest. It's nice to pick up a broad education, but there comes a point when you will want to focus your efforts on one very precise activity or idea. Be patient and try not to force it. It may require plenty of trial and error before you find that thing you "lose yourself in." That will be a sign. Go deeper!

You can learn from anyone and everyone once you start to fully appreciate this type of mindset. You start to see every person you meet as having knowledge that you could pick up and then apply to your life. This shift is powerful once you fully embrace it and what it can do for you. There is a pretty cool teacher at millennial-revolution.com.

Don't be afraid to look dumb in these daily situations we call life. You are not dumb. You are inquisitive and anxious to learn more about life and the abundance that surrounds you. This approach requires a person with a high degree of self-esteem. Work at that. Be interested enough to want more for your life. Expect more from YOU.

So, let's wrap this up with a nice little bow. It's time to grow down as you seek to understand life and yourself by playing dumb whenever possible. This challenging method requires brutal honesty with that person in the mirror. Work at finding the truth and the wisdom amongst the noise that makes up much of life. Enlightenment to follow.

"Curiosity is the essence of human existence. Who are we? Where are we? Where do we come from? Where are we going? … I don't know. I don't have any answers to those questions. I don't know what's over there around the corner. But I want to find out."

- **Eugene Cernan**

4

IS LIFE FAIR?

Life is not fair. It's important to head out into life after receiving that diploma knowing that bad things happen to good people. As one old boss once said to me, "Shit happens, Finley, get used to it." This chapter is brought to you from an old Army First Sergeant (me) who tends to shoot straight even when it might hurt a bit to hear the truth.

It is important to see the world as it is, rather than as you think it should be. This approach gets you started off on the right path with a clear understanding of the environment and all the characters found in it. The environment? The atmosphere you are entering. It is not full of rainbows, unicorns and good people at every turn.

As a matter of fact, there are many "creatures" waiting to pounce on the unsuspecting graduate. The environment is actually full of tigers, sharks and alligators who will eat you! Those are the characters that exist in that unfriendly place we call life. P.S. Tigers, sharks and alligators will appear normal to the uninformed eye so be careful out there.

So, why am I telling you this. Shit is going to hit the fan real quick after you pick up that diploma and head out into that unforgiving world. If you aren't ready to enter a world that is cruel at times, you might just find that fan turned on YOU. You must get ready mentally and physically for a place that is demanding and possibly brutal at times.

How? You're going to have to toughen up mentally. When bad things happen, accept it. Of course bad things happen. That's life and we should expect nothing different. You simply deal with those difficulties as best you can rather than running away from them. *You need to buck up.*

Buck up? It's slang for getting strong when life gets most difficult. It's easy to be strong when life is going well. The ones that are truly strong take the difficulties of life and deal with those challenges in a way that makes them tougher. That's right. You can get stronger mentally as you deal with one difficult experience after another.

So, how do you get stronger mentally? You deal with issues straight on. You don't ignore them. You don't become a victim. You don't blame others. You don't sit around feeling sorry for yourself. You stand up to your fears and become bigger through the process. You start as one person and gradually, over time, become a mentally stronger person.

Now, I know some of you talk a big game, but when difficulty comes along, you shrink from it. It's okay. I've been there. I know how that feels. It's easier to crawl up into your shell and hide from the world. Easy as that may be, it's a mistake. Do what is easy and life will be difficult. Do what is difficult and life will be easy. That's a good mantra to live by and it will serve you well as your life unfolds over time.

What doesn't kill you will make you stronger. That's another good saying that might help when life throws you a big ball of crud. Keep telling yourself that you can overcome the difficulties of life even when you're not sure you can. It is imperative that you believe in yourself and what you can do even when life is most challenging. When shit hits the fan, turn the fan off and pick up the mess. Strength to follow.

"Bad things do happen; how I respond to them defines my character and the quality of my life. I can choose to sit in perpetual sadness, immobilized by the gravity of my loss, or I can choose to rise from the pain and treasure the most precious gift I have—life itself."

- Walter Anderson

5

LOST AND CONFUSED

If you are lost and confused about your future life, join the club. Most of us are baffled about our passions, our talents, and our direction when someone hands us a diploma and says, "Good luck." It is normal to feel that way. So, what do you do when these feelings overwhelm you?

- **Reach out to people who will help you find your way with a helping hand and advice. If they are not present in your life right now, go find them in a book, blog or podcast.**

- **Avoid people who will tear you down with their words and actions. If they are part of your life right now, find ways to distance yourself from them and their negativity.**

- **Surround yourself with people who provide diverse points of view. We need to hear different points of view even when they run counter to our thoughts at the time.**

Here is a significant piece of the puzzle that can make a significant difference in your life. Your greatest teachers are almost surely not there in front of you in physical form. The people who will quite possibly help you the most in life, could be speaking to you through a book, a podcast or a blog. You must seek out wisdom. *It will not come to you.*

Amazing people are waiting to share their wisdom with you. You must venture beyond your physical world to find those people. This type of mindset requires you to be open to change so you can grow into the person you were meant to be. Only YOU can do that. Only YOU know who that person is. Only YOU can identify YOUR truth.

Once you accept the idea that you and only you know what you were meant to do with your life and who you are ultimately meant to be, you will start down the path of self-discovery. And that my friend, can be a wondrous thing. You become the creator of your life!

Here is a tip that might help some of you along your journey of life. Find what it is that you enjoy. Losing yourself in the flow of an activity is a clear sign that you are onto something important. Then, identify ways to do more of that, whatever that is. Keep these points in mind.

- **Don't worry about making money doing it.**

- **Don't worry about whether you are good or bad when doing it.**

- **Don't worry about failing when you are doing what you love.**

- **Don't worry about looking stupid as you do what feels right.**

As this book plays out, I will prod and poke you into looking within for the truth even if it makes you a bit uncomfortable. Within? *That internal soul that is yours has the answers to what will bring meaning to your life.* Keep reminding yourself of that very important message.

I will attempt to help you identify your unique path. But the real work will be done by you. It will be your job to get on your path, stay on your path, and then circle back and show others the way to find their path. It's time to be courageous. It's time to find YOU.

"The first step toward success is taken when you refuse to be a captive of the environment in which you first find yourself."

- **Mark Caine**

6

FOREVER THE STUDENT

To grow as a human being, it is important to never stop being a student. The key with that last statement is how a student is defined. Try not to limit the definition of a student to someone in a classroom. Broaden that definition to include anyone who is open to learning under all types of circumstances. That's what it means to be forever the student.

Far too many people see a diploma as the end of their education. The truth is, that diploma should play a very small part of your educational life. Expanding yourself beyond graduation day will help you achieve success in life where others do not. You realize that your growth as a human being will take place outside a classroom, not inside.

How does a person go about applying this concept? *Stop looking at brick and mortar schools as the primary place to pick up an education.* Start looking outside those buildings and classrooms as you expand on what you know and what you want to know about the world and about YOU. Where does a person go when applying this idea?

Books would be a good place to start. Your local library and online bookstores can be wonderful places to pick up an education at little to no cost. For some people, a favorite blog, podcast or app might do the trick. Next, I would be looking at Khanacademy.org. Sal Khan and his crew are teaching more people than anyone in the world and it is FREE.

You can take classes at little to no cost from online institutions like MIT, Stanford and Harvard (google them to learn more). That's right, you can learn from some wonderful teachers in the comfort of your own home and on your schedule and in many cases, it will cost you nothing!

You can watch Ted Talks ([ted.com](ted.com)) to become enlightened on one topic or another without it costing you a dime. Those videos are there to pierce your brain (and your heart) in some remarkable ways. It's worth your time to hear from people who have something important to share. Who knows, you might even be one of them one day!

There is a catch to being forever the student. You must be properly motivated to learn and that means you are ready and willing to change so you can grow. To be forever the student, you must not only be open to learning, but you need to embrace this idea of always being a student throughout your life. What do I mean by that last sentence?

You embrace the idea of learning something new every day. You understand that one concept today will help you better understand a new concept tomorrow. A chain reaction starts to occur when you layer bits of new information on top of old information. That cumulative effect over long periods of time will bring you valuable knowledge that you could not have envisioned earlier in the process.

You can use that knowledge to not only help yourself and your loved ones, but to make the world a better place. The adults in the room are right when they say education is incredibly important, but they are mistaken if they assume it only takes place in a classroom. Exit the classroom to seek the truth about life. The world is waiting to provide you vast amounts of knowledge. Go get it!

"I know that I have the ability to achieve the object of my definite purpose in life; therefore, I demand of myself persistent, continuous action toward its attainment, and I here and now promise to render such action."

- **Napoleon Hill**, *Think and Grow Rich*

7

TAKE A BREAK

Many people would be wise to take a break between high school and college or between undergraduate and graduate school as they learn more about themselves and what they want for their future life. A break? Go get a job that pays the bills. Travel with funds you have saved up. Join the military. You could even go live in the woods for two years and two months (read *Walden* to learn more).

Why should a person take a break? They are not ready for that next level of education at that time. They don't know what they want to do with their life. They haven't learned how to dedicate themselves to their studies. They are not mature enough at that time to make the most of what they are being exposed to in the classroom. There are many good reasons to take a break and you need to hear that before making that next move.

Are there pitfalls to taking a break? Sure, but I believe the pitfalls of picking up tons of debt without knowing what you want to do with your life are far worse. Taking a break could be the exact right move for many people at many different stages of their lives. Turning and going down a different path than others may just be the right decision at the right time for someone like YOU. So, what are the pitfalls of taking a break?

(1) You may never end up continuing your formal education. College may not be a place you need to go. (2) You may end up in a low skilled, low paying job. You can move on from those positions as many people have done before you. (3) You *could* end up separated from your friends. Make new friends. These are all challenges that are easily overcome by the person who learns how to think for themselves.

There is another challenge many people will encounter if they choose this path of taking a break. Mom and Dad are generally big fans of college and they may not like you taking a break. Why? They want you to get certified (diploma) so you will have more opportunities at better, higher paying jobs in the future, which should stop you from moving back and living in the basement or worse, living in a van down by the river. While those concerns are valid, they don't always make sense.

Going to college to party and pick up a lot of debt is dumb. Many people do it because they are simply not ready for that newfound freedom. Basically, it is a case of immaturity. That certainly applied to me once upon a time and it applies to many young people today. *A break can be the solution that helps you work through an impasse.* Reassure your parents that you are not eliminating college from your life, just delaying it until you find more answers. Give them a hug when you break it to them, they might need it.

Let's wrap this up. If you are lost and confused when receiving a diploma, it might be time to take a break from formalized education (never take a break from seeking knowledge). Whether it is twelve months or twelve years, you need to figure out what it is that you truly want to do with your life *without* incurring a bunch of debt at some random college. Keep your eyes open during this process. Opportunities may show up where you least expected it. That will be the time to seize the moment.

"If a man does not keep pace with his companions, perhaps it is because he hears a different drummer. Let him step to the music which he hears, however measured or far away."

- **Henry David Thoreau**

8

OPENING AND CLOSING DOORS

Many people go into deep debt so they can get a college diploma to "open doors" where they are currently closed because they lack a diploma. While it is ridiculous why that must be done, I do acknowledge the reality of the situation. A diploma does open many doors.

Many employers will not let you interview for a job without that piece of paper called a diploma. They use the diploma to whittle down the number of applicants in many situations. Is there a way to fight this process of discrimination toward people who don't have a piece of paper that says they are smart/qualified/worthy?

Yes, is my initial answer. But first, let's take a step back and review the current situation. If there is something that you really want to do like become a pediatrician who delivers babies, then yes, you will need to get all of the diplomas that industry says you must have. Certain occupations require expertise that necessitates many years inside the classroom.

We probably don't want people reading a book or two and then delivering babies full-time. The same might go for other professions that require a great deal of technical knowledge like an engineer or a dentist, but this list is smaller than it might appear to be. Many people who master their area of interest, do it without a diploma.

Do you need a diploma to be a great businessman? No. Do you need a diploma to be a great teacher? No. A great preacher? No. A great manager? No. A great police officer? No. Now, I am not saying those jobs are easy. I am just saying you don't need a diploma to perform them well. Becoming an expert at what you do has little to do with a diploma.

Most jobs can be mastered by someone with a passion for what they do, a good work ethic that gets them there on time and ready to go, an ability to work well with others (even when some of those others are a pain in the butt) and a willingness to learn from their mistakes (and others).

So, what is the solution if you are looking for a good job that pays well, but you don't have the diploma to get you in the doors that lead to opportunities? Keep working at whatever job you currently have and then start a small business on the side doing what you want to do.

Tap into that inner entrepreneur that is waiting to be released. *You could create something out of nothing.* Finding your niche to provide a service and/or product that others want is valuable and it does not require any kind of diploma in many cases.

It does require knowledge. Learn more about this subject by reading up on starting a business and how to make it prosperous for years to come. Here is a book that might help: *The 4-Hour Workweek*, by Timothy Ferriss. Learn the right methods from those that made it happen.

Becoming an entrepreneur is something anyone can do (it does take guts so make sure you have plenty of those) and with some self-education on your chosen field and plenty of hard work, you could end up leaving your job that doesn't pay much, for a small business that does.

Are there drawbacks to starting your own business? Sure, you could fall on your face. If you provide a service or make a product that people reject then that falls on you, which means you must put in the hard work to produce something of real value that others want and need. A diploma will not be the deciding factor. YOU will be.

"Starting your own business isn't just a job–it's a way of life."

- **Richard Branson**

9

WORK IS A GOOD THING

We all benefit from picking up a good work ethic as early in life as possible. There is dignity that comes with work. Whether you start working as a kid, a teenager or as a young adult; the benefit of working hard and long will serve you well in life. Success will not come without continuous effort and commitment to the job at hand. Let's look at one young person and the lessons he learned along the way.

There was once a young man who joined the military and in very short order, found himself working 12 hour days, (stretching to 16 hour days much of the time) six days a week. At first he struggled with the long, hard days, but in time, he found strength in what he was doing. Hard work taught him that life was not going to give him what he wanted, he had to go get it. That young man was me.

Work gives us a feeling of accomplishment when done right. We feel part of something and when we hit the sack at the end of the day, hopefully, we sleep well knowing we provided something of value. Work provides that feeling of achievement that is hard to receive in many other ways. Here is a key point. Finding work that teaches you these important lessons will prepare you for the difficulties ahead.

So, how does a person go about achieving a good work ethic. Start working! Find someone who will give you a job even when you lack much in the way of skills. Get in there and work hard to learn something and become better each day. Get to work early and stay late. Go beyond what is expected and show your boss how much you appreciate the opportunity that he or she has bestowed upon you. Here is something that will serve you well: *Under promise and over deliver.* Give people more than they expect.

Allow me to throw a bit of reality into the discussion. Sometimes work sucks. It is important to understand that, too. If you think every day will be blissful and full of joy, you are going to be sadly disappointed. That will not be the case and we should accept that truth as well.

You will very likely have a bad boss or two during your working life. You will have co-workers who spend too much time gossiping instead of working. You will get blamed for something that wasn't your fault. You will probably feel underpaid and unappreciated. Welcome to life.

So why did I throw those last two paragraphs in there? Because you need to hear the truth and it isn't always pretty. Life can be downright hard and we shouldn't expect it any other way. No one gets through life without getting roughed up a bit. Accept that reality and don't be surprised when things go wrong. Accept a difficult situation and push on.

You NEED to achieve a mental toughness as you mature into the adult you are going to become one day. The process helps you evolve into the person you are going to be in the future. You are tougher than you realize. Believe in yourself and do the very best you can with every task provided to you at every job location along the way.

When you feel like quitting or feeling sorry for yourself, look in the mirror and tell that person not to give up. Fail forward as you do what is needed when life gets hard. The person who keeps getting up and trying one more time will find achievement where others end in failure. Success comes to those who try one more time. Try one more time.

"The price of success is hard work, dedication to the job at hand, and the determination that whether we win or lose, we have applied the best of ourselves to the task at hand."

- **Vince Lombardi**

10

SUCCESS?

What is success? That is a difficult question to answer. Let's be clear on one key point. There is no right or wrong answer. Each person must figure this out for themselves, and by the way, that can and most likely will change over time. Why will it change? You will change.

Here is a list of *21 Suggestions for Success* by H. Jackson Brown, Jr. It's good advice and worth your time and energy. Step by step, find your own level of success in this crazy world. Believe in your ability to create the life you want and that means creating YOU along the way.

(1) Marry the right person. This one decision will determine 90% of your happiness or misery.

(2) Work at something you enjoy and that's worthy of your time and talent.

(3) Give people more than they expect and do it cheerfully.

(4) Become the most positive and enthusiastic person you know.

(5) Be forgiving of yourself and others.

(6) Be generous.

(7) Have a grateful heart.

(8) Persistence, persistence, persistence.

(9) Discipline yourself to save money on even the most modest salary.

(10) Treat everyone you meet like you want to be treated.

(11) Commit yourself to constant improvement.

(12) Commit yourself to quality.

(13) Understand that happiness is not based on possessions, power or prestige, but on relationships with people you love and respect.

(14) Be loyal.

(15) Be honest.

(16) Be a self-starter.

(17) Be decisive even if it means you'll sometimes be wrong.

(18) Stop blaming others. Take responsibility for every area of your life.

(19) Be bold and courageous. When you look back on your life, you'll regret the things you didn't do more than the ones you did.

(20) Take good care of those you love.

(21) Don't do anything that wouldn't make your Mom proud.

"It had long since come to my attention that people of accomplishment rarely sat back and let things happen to them. They went out and happened to things."

- **Leonardo da Vinci**

11

THE STORIES WE TELL

Many human beings have a way of telling stories that are just not true. Most of those stories are untruths we tell to ourselves. Be careful, those falsehoods can do great harm to you and your future. As you pick up that diploma and head off into life, be sure to understand just how many stories you know that are simply not true.

So, what exactly am I getting at with that last paragraph? I am talking about that little voice in your head that questions everything you do with lies. Lies? You are dumb. You are ugly. You are weak. And maybe the biggest one, you are a big fat failure. Those are some of the lies that make up the stories some people tell themselves.

So, how do you handle those stories that pop up throughout the day to thwart your future life? Accept the fact that others have that negative voice in their head as well. We all hear bad news, but some people can push that aside, while others find it difficult. Which one are you going to be?

A successful future depends on your ability to push those stories aside. It's not easy. Insecurity comes along for the ride, especially when we are young. The lies may change over time, but they generally have one overriding theme. You're just not good enough in one way or another. Why do we hear those stories and where did they come from?

You can look directly at the media and your surroundings. The mass media distorts life. They give you the news they want to share, and it is usually news that breeds conflict within your environment AND your head. They cause you to make judgments about yourself based on what you are seeing. Of course, what you are seeing is nothing more than a show.

The more exposure to the media (this includes old media like television, radio and movies as well as new media like Facebook and Twitter), the more lies you will end up telling yourself as you make the inevitable comparisons. The mass media and the people who promote it are putting on one big phony performance. Tune them out.

What you see coming out of the many media outlets is something that does more harm to you not only at that moment, but for decades to come. The more you expose yourself to those messages, the worse off you will be. Messages? People on the big screen are special and what they say should be followed closely. Just say no to that message.

Stop comparing yourself to others. Stop exposing yourself to the negative in society. *Focus on the good.* Emphasize what is decent and you will see the good where others do not. Send out love instead of hate and that requires you to think for yourself. It is better to struggle and fail listening to your truth than to "succeed" by living by someone else's rules.

Find that inner voice that guides you toward becoming your true self as you push aside those lies coming from the media who spend their days building people up so they can knock them down. Reduce that exposure and you will reduce the lies that bubble up from within. Basically, you learn to change the stories as you take control of your life.

Here are two books that should help you better understand your true potential: *Level up Your Life: How to Unlock Adventure and Happiness by Becoming the Hero of Your Own Story* by Steve Kamb and *Seven Times Down, Eight Times Up* by Alan Gettis. Find YOU and the lies will gradually fade into the darkness where they belong.

"Make a mental list of happy thoughts and pass them through your mind several times every day. If an unhappiness thought should enter your mind, immediately stop, consciously eject it, and substitute a happiness thought."

- **Norman Vincent Peale**, *The Power of Positive Thinking*

12

EDUCATION VS. KNOWLEDGE

Many people lump education and knowledge into one category. As early in life as possible, you want to see the vast difference between these two concepts and what they can do for you and your future. An education tends to equal formalized work like you get in a classroom. Knowledge is what happens outside that classroom as you find your way through this crazy thing we call life.

The word education is used by many people to mean many different things. Someone might say you have an education because you received some diploma from some institution. Many times, when you leave a college with one diploma or more, people think of you as being "smart." Is that right?

Some people might think knowledge is acquired in a formal classroom with some teacher lecturing on one topic or another. That's not how you acquire knowledge. Knowledge comes to those who seek the truth outside the school as they apply what they have learned elsewhere.

The classroom may serve as a place to "light the torch," but it is not a place to acquire knowledge. If all a person does, is show up, take notes, memorize the information and then feed it back to the teacher in a test, they are going to end up with little more than a diploma.

Knowledge comes to those who seek the answers to life outside the classroom. They take small bits of new information and explore those crumbs to see their depth. A simple visual would be an iceberg. The small amount of ice you see above the water might be education that is received in a classroom. The large amount of ice below the surface is the knowledge.

So, how does one acquire knowledge in their short existence on this big rock we call Earth? Not in the classroom. P.S. I picked up my college diploma at the ripe ole age of 48. It was interesting and educational, but what I learned there, is less than 1% of what I have learned outside that degree program. Here is what I have learned outside the classroom.

- **Knowledge comes to those who are curious about the world and the environments and people that occupy it.**

- **Knowledge comes to those who seek the answers to life and it's many problems, no matter the difficulties.**

- **Knowledge comes to those who want more than just someone's version of what an education is and should be.**

- **Knowledge comes to those who challenge the world they live in and what they hear all around them.**

- **Knowledges comes to those who seek it out, rather than waiting for it to show up at their doorstep.**

So, where does a person start? Go pick up a book that causes you to think critically. Here are three books you might find interesting and thought provoking: *Grit* by Angela Duckworth, *Nudge* by Richard Thaler and Cass Sunstein and *Switch* by Chip and Dan Heath. At every turn, remind yourself to seek knowledge. Enlightenment to follow!

"What we think determines what happens to us, so if we want to change our lives, we need to stretch our minds."
- **Wayne Dyer**

13

NO COLLEGE?

It is okay if you never go to college. We all need to hear that statement at least once before considering the merits of entering a college campus and seeking a degree. There are many people who have no business going to college at different stages of their lives. I include myself in that statement. Let me explain what I mean.

When I received my high school diploma, I was dumbfounded about what I wanted to do with my life, as are many in the same situation. I was searching for answers and there were certainly many people providing me advice. Many well-meaning people were telling me to go to college so I could figure out what I wanted to do. It would have been a mistake.

The truth is, in today's world, college is not a good place to figure out what you want to do with the rest of your life. Why? The debt. Taking on large amounts of debt while you try to figure out who you are and what you want to do is not a wise solution. *There is a large percentage of people who end up with a great deal of debt and no degree.* That must be avoided.

Now some of you might be thinking I am telling you to reject further education. I am not saying that at all. As a matter of fact, I encourage you to seek as much education as you can after leaving high school as you identify the knowledge that will help you recognize what you want your life to look like over the next few decades.

I just want you to avoid the debt. Consider the many options available to you outside the classroom at little to no cost. A good book could be one of your many options. *Financial Happine$$* was written for those who are at the beginning of this journey we call life.

Are you a reader? If not, become one! I did and so can you. No one is born a reader. You develop into a reader over time as you read one book after another. It starts by picking up a book with a topic that interests you. Just take it one step at a time. When the first book is complete, go to the next one. And then the next. And then next.

Reading can change your life and make you more knowledgeable than your college educated friends who may or may not end up with a piece of paper and loads of debt. A classroom does not make you smart. As a matter of fact, it can make you clueless if you stop learning once you get a diploma. Seek knowledge while others seek pieces of paper.

It is perfectly okay to take some job just to pay the bills until you figure out the right course of action. A job that appears to lead nowhere can be a good place to be temporarily until you figure things out. Stay out of debt until you better understand what you want to do with your life. Take on debt only when you have a more clear vision of your future.

It will be much less stressful and far better financially for you to avoid the debt that comes with many college diploma's. Taking out large amounts of debt to get a pretty piece of paper can be a big fat mistake for many. So, be patient with this process as you consider the many options that are available to you in today's world. Wisdom to follow.

"The books that help you most are those which make you think the most. The hardest way of learning is that of easy reading; but a great book that comes from a great thinker is a ship of thought, deep freighted with truth and beauty."
 - **Pablo Neruda**

14

LEARN AND EARN

There are many opportunities in today's world to learn and earn WITHOUT taking on large amounts of debt. Instead of going to some college and leaving with $30,000 or more of debt after five years or so with limited job possibilities, you could have $30,000 or more worth of savings, no debt, and a job waiting for you after the five years. Would you be interested in a deal like that?

There are many apprenticeship programs where someone or an organization will pay you as they teach you. You learn and earn at the same time. A trade school could be one option for many people looking to expand on what they know without taking on vast amounts of debt doing it. Why go into deep debt if you don't have to? There are some awesome jobs out there for those who are interested in seeking them out.

You could learn and earn as you become a welder, electrician, graphic designer, big equipment operator, computer programmer, police officer, paralegal, fire fighter, plumber, web developer, diesel mechanic, commercial diver, aircraft mechanic, multimedia animator, dental hygienist, and many, many jobs in the medical field. The options are truly unlimited for those who are open to the many possibilities.

So, where does a person start? Educate yourself on the many options out there and what you may enjoy doing with your future. Go to profoundlydisconnected.com. This site belongs to Mike Rowe (the guy who made dirty jobs cool). Mike provides scholarships to those who are interested in learning a skill and mastering a trade. There are many options for those who are ready and willing to work hard toward improving their future AND improving their financial picture to boot.

Here is another option. Go to college, receive a degree, get paid to do it, pick up no debt and when you graduate, you have a job waiting for you. It's called ROTC and every Military Branch offers it in one form or another throughout the United States. There are many opportunities to do many different things within the ROTC program based on the course of study you select. Opportunities abound.

Now, there is a catch to everything I just discussed. It does require plenty of effort and hard work on your part. Basically, you will get out of these programs, what you put into them. Here is what I know. You can pick up an education on many different subjects, AND another diploma, AND a job, AND do it while incurring little to no debt. Why would someone not consider those options?

It seems like too much work? No, it's not. You won't get to go to college with your friends? Maybe not, but you can console them years later when they are deep in debt and looking for a job, while you have no debt and enjoy your job and your future opportunities. You won't make as much money as your average college graduate? Maybe, maybe not. There are many college graduates making something close to minimum wage.

What about those people who say everyone should go to college? They are wrong and should be pushed aside. Thousands of people are not ready for college and that is perfectly okay. There are many wonderful options for you to get an education, gather knowledge, and put your life on a good path going forward without picking up a ton of debt. Believe in that and believe in YOU.

"The greatest discovery of any generation is that human beings can alter their lives by altering the attitudes of their minds."

- Albert Schweitzer

15

THE MILITARY

DO NOT SKIP THIS CHAPTER. I realize many of you have no interest in the military. Once upon a time, I didn't either, but before you shove this idea aside, I would like you to hear me out on this valuable option. It could be exactly the right move for many young men and women based on their current circumstances.

Why the military? They will take individuals with little to no skills, pay you well with good benefits, teach you skills that you cannot imagine right now, provide a FREE college education (or help pay for one you already got), introduce you to amazing people and places, and maybe most importantly, the military provides the structure that many of us need at such a young age (that included me).

Here are a couple of ways to look at this subject. You could join up and serve full time on active duty for a period of years like four or six (enlisted or as an officer). You could also join up and serve in the National Guard or Reserves in a part-time status to help pay the bills, supplementing full-time income from your job in "civilian life." These options provide you the chance to serve your country in ways most people will not. That can be reason enough to join the military. Next up, what branch?

The Marines? The Army? The Navy? The Air Force? The Coast Guard? I would recommend you explore all branches to see what they offer and where your interests lie. There is no right answer on this issue and do not let others (including a recruiter) tell you otherwise. The key lies in understanding your choices and your interests and then seeing what each branch is offering at that time. P.S. Keep in mind that it can change dramatically based on current world affairs.

What are the drawbacks to being in the military? (1) You could end up in a war. Let's go ahead and get that out there on the table. That is possible. (2) You will be entering a world where people give you orders and your job will be to follow them. (3) You will lose a degree of freedom (you can't just walk away with no consequences). (4) The people in charge of you will not be as sweet and forgiving as mom. That is actually a good thing. You will grow up quickly in the military.

The military also separates you from parents and loved ones and forces you to confront life head on. While this can be quite scary (it was for me), I would tell you this could be the right move as it helps you stand up and deal with life and its many difficulties. The military forces you to figure out solutions when life becomes difficult. *You learn to take responsibility for yourself, as you learn to save yourself rather than hoping others will do it for you.*

In the big scheme of things, the pluses of the military far outweigh the negatives. The military takes young people and turns them into adults. It did that for me and it can do it for you. Here is one final piece of advice. Each person's experience in the military is different based on what they do, where they are, and who they are with. The military is not one way. It is many ways. Keep your options open.

"All life demands struggle. Those who have everything given to them become lazy, selfish, and insensitive to the real values of life. The very striving and hard work that we so constantly try to avoid is the major building block in the person we are today."

- **Pope Paul VI**

16

THE PARENTS

Most parents are good people. They want what is best for their children in most cases. The question is, "Do they know what is best for their children?" Maybe they do and maybe they don't. Now, before I get a bunch of hate mail from some parents, let me explain.

Most parents want their children to be good people. That means getting a good job that pays well, making a positive difference in the world, not hurting anyone, working hard, and finding someone to share it with. Throw in a good religious background, a few kids and you might call it a day if their offspring accomplished everything on that list.

What happens if the child goes in a different direction than what the parents want? Instead of getting a good job that pays well, they get a great job that doesn't pay all that much. They can still make a difference in the world. They can still not hurt anyone. And they can still work hard. Will that suffice for the parents?

What happens if the child ends up with a different religion (or no religion) than their parents? Will that go over well? I seriously doubt it. Most parents think they have the whole religion thing figured out and so the child should fall in line (this is a rather universal idea, whether you live in the United States, Saudi Arabia, India, China, Peru, Israel, etc.).

So, what am I getting at with this chapter? At some point, each one of us should start thinking instead of copying. We must decide what we believe in and what we don't believe in. *We stop thinking like our parents and start thinking for ourselves.* We tell mom and dad that we are ready to do our own critical thinking on the big issues of the day.

Now, some of you reading this chapter will say, "Hell yeah!" You are ready to tell your parents to butt out of your life. Don't go too fast. What you think and do could be wrong! There are consequences to your actions and in the end, it will be you who must answer for what you do.

There are others of you who are not ready to challenge their parents. You *allow* mom and dad to do the thinking for you. That is certainly an option, but it is no way to find meaning in your life. Meaning comes in life from doing what you want, not what others want for you.

The truth is, the issue is a difficult one and you must figure things out as you go along. You are wise to listen to your parents in many cases as you progress through your early years. But at some point, you might need to challenge the people and environment that raised you.

The only way you are going to know that is to explore beyond your safe and sheltered environment. It will take courage to live a life that is truly yours and you should not expect it to be easy. You will fail at times. You will find out that mom and dad weren't so dumb after all, but also, that they didn't have all the answers.

If you want to find the answers to a meaningful life, you must take the call to adventure per the guidance of Joseph Campbell. There will be more on Mr. Campbell later in the book. In the meantime, be brave and think for yourself whenever possible. Ultimately, that is how you end up with a life worth living.

"I believe that one defines oneself by reinvention.

    To not be like your parents. To not be like your friends.

        To be yourself. To cut yourself out of stone."

- **Henry Rollins**

17

THE LEADER

Are you a follower or a leader? How you answer that question will tell us plenty about your future. Followers end up doing what others want them to do. They don't do what they want to do. Leaders do their own thing. They identify what is right for them and then they do it. And, if people don't like it, they wave their hand and keep on going.

Many people are followers. They seem to be okay with that, but I don't know why. There is no great ending for the follower. They end up living someone else's version of what their life should be. They fail to follow their own compass because they are too busy following someone else's. Here is the good news for followers: *Followers can become leaders.*

Why would you want to become a leader? You get to live out your dreams instead of someone else's. You get the opportunity to explore life on your own terms instead of someone else's. You get to the end of your life and say: "I did it my way; failures and all." It's worth it to become a leader, but it's also hard in many cases.

Hard? Leaders tend to stick out from the crowd. Conformity is a dirty word in their language. Many people don't like it when you separate from the group. They might call you names and shun you. They might challenge you in ways that may cause fear to creep into your mind. Being a leader is difficult, but it's worth it.

There is no way you are going to find your true self in life by following other people's paths. You must find your path and yours alone. A path no one has walked. A path that may be lonely at times, but a path that will lead to a better understanding of YOU.

The importance of becoming a leader lies in *allowing yourself* to do what you believe is right even when others don't. Your internal compass will tell you what direction to take. Leaders also encourage others to find their path as they fight for the freedoms of others just as he or she has battled to achieve those freedoms for themselves.

The great leaders help others embark on their own journey toward finding meaning and fulfillment in their lives. Take some time to learn about Mohandas Gandhi and the fourteenth Dalai Lama. Those are two amazing leaders who improved the lives of millions of people. What about someone close to home? Look at John Bogle. Now, that is a leader!

So, where does one start? Start with the belief in yourself. You can become a leader. Tell that to the person in the mirror as many times as necessary until it "sticks." It starts with belief. Next up, find leaders in your everyday life and/or in the history books.

Learn from the successful so you can be successful. They leave a trail that you and I can study. This attitude requires the development of the right habits and behaviors over time that will help you become the person you want to be. Every day is an opportunity to learn and grow.

Be patient with the process. Becoming a great leader takes time and there will be plenty of ups and downs along the way. Here are two books that can help: *Leadership Gold*, by John C. Maxwell and *Losing My Virginity*, by Richard Branson. The answers are out there. Go find them!

"Do not go where the path may lead, go instead where there is no path and leave a trail."

- **Ralph Waldo Emerson**

18

THE PRESIDENT

The President of the United States has less of an impact on your life than you do. I want you to hear that message loud and clear because you will hear many adults in your life complaining in one way or another about how the current President is hurting them. The results of your life will flow from you, not the President.

Let's take a step back to clearly explain this point. Whether the President (whoever that may be) supports what you find to be important (gay marriage for example) or doesn't support what you think is important (gun rights for example), there isn't much you're going to do about that and you shouldn't lose much sleep over it either.

The President will not have a big impact on your life based on their rhetoric (politicians talk a lot, but action doesn't always follow the words). Even if they do get the rest of the politicians to go along with what they want (hard to do when the government is divided along party lines), it will usually be a negotiation that ends up "watering down" the issue.

The point is this: You and I should not stress out over what some politician says even if he or she is sitting in the White House. In the big scheme of things, the United States and its economy is much bigger than one person. We don't live under a dictatorship. Don't waste your precious life energy reacting to politicians; no matter what their position.

Now, at this point, I know some people would challenge what I am saying. They think politicians are very important to our lives. This belief causes many people to give large amounts of time, energy and sometimes money to some person who tells them what they want to hear.

I wouldn't do that if I was you. Politicians do not run the United States. People run the United States. People elect politicians. Politicians do not elect the people. Most politicians simply take the pulse of the crowd and then tell them what they want to hear. What they do once in office can be something very different from what they ran on during a campaign.

Presidents are no different. They just happen to be the politician that gets the most headlines due to the position they are trying to weasel their way into. In the big picture that makes up your life, the current President is a blip on the screen. Focus more on YOUR thinking and actions, not on what the President is saying or doing.

YOU are the person who will have a very big impact on your life going forward. Everything you do from one minute to the next will have consequences attached to it. Blaming the President or seeing the President as some kind of savior will get you nowhere. It is critically important for you to recognize the true savior of your future life. It is YOU.

The President of the United States is just some person who happens to have a big stage with a big bullhorn that reaches millions and maybe billions of people all over the world. Push the talk aside and get on with your life. Focus your efforts on what you can do and believe me, you can do plenty. Start NOW by creating YOUR life.

"The big divide in this country is not between Democrats and Republicans, or women and men, but between talkers and doers."

- **Thomas Sowell**

19

THE SIGNIFICANT OTHER

Any person you invite into your life will have an impact on your life. How big of an impact? It could be HUGE based on who that person is, the time and place they enter and what they bring with them. This chapter has a lot to do with understanding the importance of having a significant other (or not) at those critical moments that make up your life.

When we are young, we tend to select mates for less than ideal reasons. Many guys are looking for the prettiest girl in the room and many ladies are looking for the big manly stud who can protect them and their future children. There are a whole lot of hormones involved and that can lead to some pretty big mistakes.

Mistakes? Getting married to someone because of what they look like is a mistake. Looks fade, but many issues, including high levels of debt (and the behaviors that lead a person into that situation) and the stress that comes with it, can stay with you forever. Patience is required prior to selecting someone to marry or live with.

Now, I am not trying to play marriage counsellor. I am no more qualified than the next guy in telling you who you should marry and who you shouldn't. What I am saying is that you had better consider what life will be like once the lovey dovey stage passes. Will that person be a good partner for decades to come?

Let's be honest about the issue. It's almost impossible to tell how that other person will turn out in ten years or so. It's hard enough to figure ourselves out, let alone someone else. Take your time and don't be in a hurry when selecting a mate. *People change a lot over the years.*

In many cases, couples do not grow in the same direction and at the same speed. The scenario plays out in a very familiar way. Two people fall in love and the next step seems logical to many. Let's get married! Maybe the next step should be, let's spend a few years with each other to see if we really want to spend the rest of our lives together.

You have little control over who you fall in love with, but in most parts of the world, you have full control when it comes to who you marry. It's important to acknowledge this key point. Just because you fall in love with someone, doesn't mean you should marry them. Infatuation should not be the driving force toward getting married.

It will take you many years to figure out who you are and what you want to be. It is a process that takes time. For some people, they think a marriage partner will speed that up and make life great. That is unlikely. There are married people who are happy and there are married people who are miserable. Marriage is not a solution to achieving happiness.

What is? If only it was so simple that it could be summarized in a few words. I certainly do not have all of the answers, but here is a tip. Stop looking for someone else to make you happy. The person who can make you happy is that person in the mirror. There lies your answer.

It would be wise to put in the time on your own self-development prior to seeking the company of that significant someone. Here are two books that that can make a difference: *Your Erroneous Zones* by Wayne Dyer and *The Happiness Solution* by Alan Gettis. The answer lies with YOU.

"I don't take relationships too seriously, but everybody else seems to. When you get your heart broken, it's like the end of the world. I look at it as that was one moment in your life, one chapter. That person helped you grow and figure out what kind of person you want to be with in the future."

- **Colbie Caillat**

20

PHYSICALLY AND MENTALLY PRESENT

It will be very important that you stay physically and mentally present as you leave that formal classroom and enter the "world." I think most of you know what I mean by this statement, but it probably is worth reviewing for those who are unsure.

To be physically and mentally present is to not only show up in the physical form, but mentally as well. We have all been guilty (some more than others) of being present physically, but mentally we are "checked out" and nowhere to be found. Focusing the mind can change your life.

Maybe you are thinking about what you are going to do later that night. Maybe you are contemplating life after school. Who knows, maybe you are daydreaming about being some Superhero saving the world or a damsel in distress waiting to be saved by some Prince Charming.

If you are one of those people who spends plenty of time checked out, it's time to check in. How? Keep working at finding what it is that will hold your attention. I realize technology is not helping on this matter. *You MUST pull yourself away from that device and get mentally in the game.*

Start, stop, and start again can serve you well. So, what am I talking about? You start doing something that you find interesting. After a bit, that thing you did will either hold your attention mentally or it won't. If it doesn't, stop doing it and do something else. Just don't take this idea too far. Don't quit on something until you have given it a fair amount of time and energy. Continue down this path of start, stop and start until you find yourself in a state of what has been called flow.

What is flow? You find yourself in a state where hours go by like they were minutes. Time flies because you are so engrossed in what you are doing. The start, stop, and start again method gives you the opportunity to find flow in your life. When you find it, keep doing what it was that caused you flow. You might be surprised by what it could lead to.

Now, some of you might have some questions and/or concerns about this idea. When should you implement this start, stop and start again method? NOW is the right answer. There is no better time in your life than right now to start finding what it is that will bring you more happiness and meaning in your life. Get in the game!

What about your job if you have one? You keep doing your job. You either find time at the workplace (not always possible) or outside the workplace in your quest for flow. Your great awakening is almost surely going to happen on your own time.

Great things don't happen to people. Great things happen because of what people do for themselves. The point being, you must be the initiator of your life and not wait for life to come to you with its many opportunities. Focus on doing great work when possible and that means distancing yourself from other activities when necessary.

Documentaries can be good places to help you see what you currently do not. The answers to a meaningful life have been discovered by some pretty amazing people. Go find them! Here are three wonderful videos that can be found on Netflix or at one of the online bookstores: *Finding Joe*, *I AM*, and *Happy*. It's time to get mentally in the game!

"When one door of happiness closes, another opens; but often we look so long at the closed door that we don't see the one that has opened for us."

- **Henry Ford**

21

EXTERNAL VS. INTERNAL

Does the external temperature affect your internal temperature? What? Evaluate what external factors have control over your internal state and learn to choose not to let those factors influence you in a negative way. As we explore this issue in more depth, please be open and honest with that person in the mirror as we explore what lies within and how you are affected by the many external events happening around you.

First, a simple example. Let's start with the temperature as it relates to the weather and your personality. If the temperature outside is 5 degrees, does that affect your internal well-being? Does the extreme cold make you feel badly? What about a snow storm that limits what you can do outside? How about a rainstorm that cancelled the outdoor party? Think about those questions as we proceed forward.

Allowing the external to affect your internal is a choice and it is important for you to know that right here and right now. If you feel badly because of the weather outside, you made that decision. The weather did not make that decision for you. It's not the weather's fault that you feel like crap. The weather doesn't sit around trying to make you mad. It is very important that you pick up on this concept as early in life as possible. Why?

The external in life is something you and I have very little control over. Much of life is out of our control. What we do have control over, is our reaction and attitude toward what happens to us in life. It comes down to how we respond to life's events when they come crashing down on us. Bad things happen to good people and that's just the way life is. The question is, "How will YOU react to those events?"

So, where does a person go from here? Start down the path of understanding the self. Take time to get to know who you are and why you respond to life in one way or another. Why do you get angry? Why do you stress out? What brings you joy? You need to dig deep to get down to the truth as you answer those questions.

You can create a protective shield around you from the outside world. That's right. You can insulate yourself from being devastated by the bad things that will happen in your life. You have the ability to take the bad that happens to you and turn it into awareness. You end up creating your life instead of letting the environment create it for you.

You cannot stop many of the bad things from happening, but you can find that place within that will provide the peace you so desperately want, especially when life becomes difficult. Get yourself to that place of tranquility and life will become much less stressful AND more satisfying. Finding inner peace should be your ultimate goal.

The teachers are out there waiting to assist you. Here are two books that might help: *Mindset* by Carol Dweck and *The Subtle Art of Not Giving a F*ck* by Mark Manson. Both of those books are guides that take you down a path of self-discovery that goes far beyond the mundane life that surrounds you. A life of meaning and fulfillment to follow.

"Remember that the first element of all change is awareness. Watch yourself, become conscious, observe your thoughts, your fears, your beliefs, your habits, your actions, and even your inactions. Put yourself under a microscope. Study yourself."

- **T. Harv Eker**, *Secrets of the Millionaire Mind*

22

FAME AND AWARDS

Run away from fame and awards. You don't need them and you shouldn't even want them. They will lead you astray from what is really important in life. Fame and awards are external prizes that belong to people who are seeking the approval of others. Go a different route. The only person you need to impress is that person in the mirror.

Let's start with fame. Many people chase after fame. They think it will make their life better as they receive attention from other people who follow them. *It will make it worse in many cases.* We see famous people on the big screen and television and think, "That could be me." Here is what we should be saying, "I'm glad that's not me!"

What is so great about fame? Having people who you don't know follow you around to get a glimpse of you or an autograph is not my version of the good life. Having millions of people tune in to hear what you say or do means nothing. They don't know you. They only know of you and that means zilch in many cases.

I realize that some of you are not going to be easily convinced on this issue. You look at the Kardashians and other foolish celebrities and think that looks awesome. It's not. People who make a living being celebrities live shallow, meaningless lives. Ignore their antics.

We should not want to be them; we should pity them. That's right, the famous are living lives that no one should want to live. They will grow old having accomplished nothing of real value. I strongly encourage you to reject a life of fame and all that comes with it as you seek true meaning in life. Fame is the prize that you should not want to receive.

What about awards? There is a nuance here so let me be clear as I explain the subject. Working hard and achieving success in your selected field is something to be proud of and applauded. Working hard to receive some award beyond the intrinsic reward is meaningless and not worth chasing. Basically, the trophy is pointless after the achievement.

Here is an example: Some person wins some type of competition in their particular field. Good for them. The true reward will be the hard work that went into achieving that result. The journey it took to succeed at the highest level made it worthwhile. The empty award would be some type of trophy, ring, or other type of external offering that followed.

Consider this possibility. You have been brainwashed by others into thinking the ultimate reward is the external prize. I am simply trying to help you unlearn that erroneous idea so you can head out into the world with a better understanding of what really matters in life.

Let's wrap this up and move on. I ask you to trust me when I tell you that seeking fame and awards will lead to an unhappy and empty life. Learning this lesson when you are young and starting out will save you from chasing the false promises as you age.

Even if you get the fame and awards, you still lose. So, don't chase them and don't let others fool you into chasing them. Focus on the intrinsic value when striving to achieve your goals. In the end, that is what will bring you the most happiness and inner peace.

"The grass is always greener on the other side—until you get there and see it's AstroTurf. Symbols are never reality. Someone might have amassed material success and fame, but that doesn't mean they're happy. So, don't go judging a person's life by the cover."
- **Karen Salmansohn**

23

TRAVEL

One area of great interest I see with many young people is the desire to travel and see the world. I applaud you for wanting to leave your borders (physically and mentally) to discover what else is out there in this very big world of ours. Travelling can bring something to your life that is hard to explain, but it can feel oh so good. The big question is, "Should you do it with your savings or on credit?"

Let's start with a pretty simple approach to this issue. If you have the cash and you want to travel the world, go for it. You will surely grow in many wonderful ways as you experience life far beyond your present location. I personally would not take all my cash to do it, but that is your call if you want to empty your bank account to see other lands and people that inhabit them.

What does a person do if they don't have the cash? Do they borrow money to travel? Many people do and many people are broke. DO NOT borrow money to travel. If you do not have the cash, be patient, save your money, and wait until you can afford your travels. Will that delay the trips? Yes, it probably will. A bit of patience is required and while that may not be easy when you are young, it can be achieved.

So, is this issue as simple as yes with cash and no without it. I think it is. Saying all of that, there are other ways to see the world even if you have no cash saved up. Here are some options: The Peace Corp, the military, government work in a different state or overseas, a traveling nurse, pilot, flight attendant, truck driver, etc. You can even travel on nothing, finding money along the way (a bit dangerous in my mind, but it has been done by many), and here is one other option, read a book.

A book? You can travel outside your town, your state, your country, and even the planet, with a book. Refer to these trips as mental vacations if you like. You could visualize yourself in many places as your imagination runs wild with a great book. *Imagination can set you free.*

This mental approach to travel can be quite effective and inexpensive for those who are in the process of saving their money for that next physical trip. Some of you may not quite buy into this idea of a mental vacation without you ever leaving your physical surroundings. I understand.

I probably would not have received this type of message very well after picking up my high school diploma at age 18. I would have received it loud and clear, after the college diploma at age 48. I am here to tell you; a mental vacation is available to those who are ready to become readers.

This issue of travel is on the minds of millions of people who receive a degree. I get it. I encourage you to travel and see new lands and people. You will grow as a human being through the process and there is no amount of wealth that can equal that effect.

You will most likely become a better person as you enter worlds that are different from your own. Just don't limit your possibilities. There are many ways to travel physically AND mentally. Keep your options available and your mind wide open. The great unknown awaits you.

"The individual has always had to struggle to keep from being overwhelmed by the tribe. If you try it, you will be lonely often, and sometimes frightened. But no price is too high to pay for the privilege of owning yourself."

- **Friedrich Nietzsche**

24

THE KEYSTONE HABIT

It is important to identify and follow through on some keystone habits in your life. What is a keystone habit? The keystone habit is a habit that you develop over time that not only changes what you are doing in one area of your life, but it changes other parts of your life as well. Changing one habit can have life altering affects!

It would be wise to read Charles Duhigg's book, *The Power of Habit*, to better understand this amazing idea. This is a BIG deal. Focusing on changing one small habit can end up changing an entire life. That is pretty damn remarkable when you think about it. Let's explore the issue in detail so you have a clear understanding of how it all works.

Let's start with a habit, or lack thereof. You don't exercise because you haven't the time, energy, facility, ability, etc. You decide that you are going to throw all those excuses away and start by doing something small. You do 10 pushups every day when you wake up. P.S. *Changing your mindset is the #1 keystone habit based on the research.*

After one month, you start doing 15 pushups a day. In the meantime, you end up eating fewer desserts and stop drinking soda. Also, you are more efficient at work and you seem to get along better with some of your peers. Two months later, you ask the boss for more responsibilities. One year later you get a raise and you're running 3 miles a day!

The keystone habit that started that chain reaction was 10 pushups. Can it be that simple? Yes, it can. The key is in finding out what you can do right now in some small way that you can sustain. Don't worry about what it will lead to. Just do that thing (10 pushups) every day.

Of course, the same can be done with your financial situation. You sign up for your 401(k) with 3% going into your investments to get the matching funds. The money is taken out automatically and you hardly miss it. You look at your account a few months later and see your money making money in ways you never thought possible.

This "small win" makes you think about saving a bit more in your 401(k) with a few minor changes in your lifestyle. You start to cut out a coffee or two during the week and maybe bring your lunch every Monday, instead of eating out with the group. These changes end up leading to other positive happenings in your life.

You lose a couple of pounds based on eating a bit healthier. This makes you think about increasing your workout an extra 15 minutes every night and pretty soon big changes start happening in many parts of your life as those small wins keep accumulating along the way.

Soon, you are saving 10% a month and thinking about early retirement. The keystone habit can help you in many parts of your life. That's the amazing part of the whole concept. You don't have to fix everything, just focus on one thing. You might just see a whole new YOU.

"Hundreds of habits influence our days—they guide how we get dressed in the morning, talk to our kids, and fall asleep at night; they impact what we eat for lunch, how we do business, and whether we exercise or have a beer after work. Each of them has a different cue and offers a unique reward. Some are simple and others are complex, drawing upon emotional triggers and offering subtle neurochemical prizes. But every habit, no matter its complexity, is malleable. The most addicted alcoholics can become sober. The most dysfunctional companies can transform themselves. A high school dropout can become a successful manager."

- **Charles Duhigg**, *The Power of Habit*

25

DEAR MICHAEL

I have reflected for quite some time now on what I would say to myself if I could go back in time and speak to young Michael when I got that first diploma from high school. Well, here is the unvarnished advice I would provide to myself at the ripe ole age of 18.

It's okay to be scared. You should be. The world is a scary place and it is full of unknowns. Just don't let that fear stop you from trying new things. When you feel that fear bubble up inside of you, press forward and do what scares you. That's how you grow bigger and stronger.

You are not ready for college and the commitment that requires. You and I both know that. Take this opportunity to grow up before you decide to enter a classroom again. The military will be a good opportunity for you to mature into being a man. Will it be hard and scary? Damn straight it will. It will require courage. Press on.

Your true education will take place outside the classroom. Gather as much knowledge as you can. The diploma is not the end; it is only the beginning. Start reading books. Don't worry about the topic for right now. Just read about people or ideas that you find interesting. Your interests will develop over time as you develop into the person you were meant to be.

Start learning as much as you can about finances. DO NOT delay. Every decision you make on money will have a big impact on your future. Learn from the true experts on the subject and not the salespeople or the idiotic pundits on television. Start with Jane Bryant Quinn, Eric Tyson, Jonathon Clements, John Bogle, Daniel Solin, William Bernstein, Burton Malkiel, Charles Ellis, Larry Swedroe and Rick Ferri.

Focus your efforts on working well with others. It will have a big impact on your life. Learning how to deal with people and environments that are very different from you will make you a better worker, leader and person. Take the time to understand that we live in a very big world and there are many ways to live life, not one. Be more open to that idea as you appreciate the differences between people and places.

You are going to make mistakes in life. Sometimes you will make dumb decisions and you will look back and wonder why you did what you did. It's okay. You are human and everyone makes mistakes. Take full responsibility for those mistakes and learn from them. The same goes for others. Cut them some slack and give them another chance.

Surround yourself with the right people and discard the wrong influences as you step out into the world. This is extremely important and it requires a great deal of self-awareness as you make one decision instead of another with individuals and groups. The right people will build you up as you avoid the wrong people who will tear you down.

Reject the trophies and other rewards. You don't need them or the people who dangle them in front of you as some type of prize. External rewards don't matter much. The struggle will be your prize as you spend your days figuring out who you are going to be. If you are good with that person in the mirror, then you are good. It is that simple.

There will be times in life when things go terribly wrong. Hang in there and stay positive even when it seems impossible. Push negativity, hate and anger aside. Ultimately, life returns to you what you give to it. Focus on spreading as much love, compassion and forgiveness that you can. This all comes down to being the creator of your life. Make it wonderful!

"Always do your best. What you plant now, you will harvest later."

- **Og Mandino**

FINANCES

AFTER

GRADUATION

26

FINANCIAL FREEDOM

I believe financial freedom should be one of your goals. It will provide you the opportunities to do what you love as you chase your passions. It simply requires you to dedicate yourself to the steps necessary to get there. Those steps will be described in this section of the book. Follow them and financial freedom could be yours.

Financial freedom has provided me the opportunity to sit down and share what I have learned with you, so one day, you will have the chance to share your knowledge with others. People who lack this freedom are stuck in many cases, doing what they must do instead of what they want to do. Read *Graduation!* to better understand the process.

What is financial freedom? Here is how I define it. You do what you think is the best work you can do on your schedule, instead of someone else's. You don't work. You live! You create. You become the best version of yourself. Financial freedom gives you the chance to live out your dreams as you chase your passions.

Financial freedom is a wonderful place, but it doesn't happen overnight. It will take time so patience is required along this journey. It requires you to create wealth slowly over time, pushing aside the charlatans who tell you how to get rich fast. You get poor fast. You get rich slowly.

This journey of financial freedom is not necessarily easy. If it was, everyone would do it. It takes a person who is totally committed to the process and believes in themselves. You must want it so badly that you are willing to give up other things in your life that interest you. Sacrifice is required for those who want financial freedom.

Do you want it? A resounding YES is needed. If you hesitated or if you said something like, "sure," it probably isn't going to happen for you. You must be "all in" to make financial freedom a reality. At times, you will have to stand up to friends and family when they question what you are doing. Demonstrate your courage when those times come.

Others might not understand your commitment to this thing called financial freedom. They want you to have a life similar to what they are living. I am not even sure what that means to some people, but if it means living paycheck to paycheck forever and doing what others want you to do, I would pass on that option.

Financial freedom comes to those who set their goals high and then set out on a course to achieve them as they take action where needed. The person who stays focused on the prize, *freedom to live life on your terms and on your schedule*, will get there with a bit of time and patience. Others may run faster, but they can get confused and end up lost.

You could almost see this issue through the story of the tortoise and the rabbit. Be the tortoise who moves slowly, but steadily down the right path, doing the right things at the right times. Avoid being the rabbit who jumps around in a frenetic manner only to get lost and confused along the way. Financial freedom to follow.

"Who you were yesterday need have very little bearing on who you are today or who you will be tomorrow. It is natural to evolve, to grow, to be born again. The non-literal or metaphorical view or reincarnation suggest that you can have many incarnations in this lifetime. You are not a static entity. Even if you have had a long period of stagnation or dormancy, you are still capable of changing or re-inventing yourself. Opportunities to find deeper powers within ourselves come when life seems most challenging."

- **Allan Gettis**

27

GETTING STARTED

There is no better time than right now to get started with your financial education. When I say now, I mean this very minute. Time can be your friend or your enemy. Make it your friend. You have no money? So, what. You don't need money to learn about managing it wisely. You want to start as early in life as possible so, when you do start making good money, you know exactly what to do with it.

Where? Start with *Financial Happine$$*. The book is available in paperback, e-book, or audio book. It will help you understand the world of money as it connects to finding the kind of meaning and happiness we all seek. Go to thecrazymaninthepinkwig.com to start immediately. Simply hit on the menu in the right corner of the website and the links will drop down. It's all FREE. Knowledge to follow.

Why should you focus on your financial education? The world is a big place and there are many highly trained salespeople out there waiting to get their hands on your money. A financial education helps you to level that playing field so you can keep most of your hard-earned cash. Knowledge on the subject will set you free. A lack of knowledge will send you and your money in the wrong direction.

One piece of the puzzle many people seem to gloss over is how important a financial education is toward helping you avoid the many pitfalls. Eliminating big mistakes will help you avoid losing a great deal of time, energy and money digging your way out of the "craters" you never saw coming. That is a BIG deal. Older people know this because they have fallen in their own massive craters. You want to maneuver your way around them to evade what others have not.

Will some people make fun of you for learning about money? Maybe, but that is their problem, not yours. In many cases, people make fun of people who are doing something of value that they are not. Don't let that bother you and if it does, learn to let that kind of stuff roll off your back. That is nothing but ignorance trying to rain on your parade. See one approach by someone closer to your age at millenialmoneyman.com.

There are many examples from our past of people doing what they loved even when others found them to be odd. I am sure people made fun of Warren Buffett (the greatest investor of our time). Did that stop him? Of, course not. He knew what he loved and he kept doing it. There are plenty of examples beyond the financial world.

I am betting people made fun of Bill Gates and Steve Jobs once upon a time for being nerds who spent all their time on those "stupid" computers. Did it stop them? Hell, no. Do what will bring you more freedom in your future. That my friend, will be a financial education followed by action as you do what is in your best interest.

The only person in your life that you have to impress is that individual staring back at you in the mirror. Once you fully except that basic idea, you will learn to seek knowledge on many topics without concerning yourself with other people's approval. What you sow today, you will harvest in your future. The future begins right now. Start planting!

"Your time is limited, so don't waste it living someone else's life. Don't be trapped by dogma—which is living with the results of other people's thinking. Don't let the noise of others' opinions drown out your own inner voice. And most important, have the courage to follow your heart and intuition."
- **Steve Jobs**

28

THE FIRST BIG JOB

The day will come for most of you when you finally get a decent job with an awesome paycheck either out of high school or college. You will see more money on your pay stub then you ever thought possible. Your ship has come in or so it appears.

At that very moment, you have some big decisions to make. How big? *The decisions you make at that time can decide what your future will look like for decades to come.* Is that big enough for you? Let's look at two very real options most of you will have.

Option #1: Go on a spending spree. Start buying everything you don't have and want by putting each purchase on a payment plan using credit cards and loans as you focus on monthly payments rather than the total amount of the debt and the interest rate attached to it.

What will this get you? You will look fabulous, but you will be more broke than before the spending spree. What? You just bought a bunch of depreciating assets that lost value immediately after the purchase and will continue losing value going forward.

You have just set yourself up to live paycheck to paycheck for the foreseeable future and maybe for the rest of your life. Basically, you just screwed yourself in ways that may not be immediately clear to you now, but will be in a few short years.

You took a difficult situation (some debt that is manageable) and made it much worse (a boatload of debt that is hard to manage). Millions of Americans select this option to their detriment. Will you?

Option #2: You pause when seeing that big paycheck and do something your friends don't do. You buy nothing until you put together a plan. A plan? A plan to pay down your debt and save and invest for your future needs. This requires someone who is ready and willing to think differently from the crowd.

Will you look less successful than your mall loving friends who own the latest and greatest outfits, phones, computers and vehicles? Yes, you probably will, but so what. You have a plan leading to freedom as you reduce your debt on depreciating assets (stuff) and increase your wealth on appreciating assets like stocks and bonds.

This approach to life comes down to thinking and behaving differently in very specific ways. Do you want to be rich or act rich? I hope you find that question silly. The informed person knows the difference and steers clear of the wrong path, while they get on the right path.

You can learn more on this issue by reading three of Thomas Stanley's wonderful books, *The Millionaire Next Door*, *The Millionaire Mind* and *Stop Acting Rich*. Financial freedom will belong to those who challenge the world around them. Become that person!

"America is a nation of excesses. And these excesses, especially when it comes to consumption, have a profound influence upon our young. They are constantly told that spending is the American way. Often their role models are highly compensated professional athletes and entertainers. Day after day, the public relations machinery keeps cranking out stories about the multimillion dollar mansions that this athlete has purchased or the fleet of exotic cars that this movie star owns. By sensationalizing and glorifying these powerful role models, the press sends a message. It says that happiness is obtained by spending freely on cars, homes, and parties. But in reality, spending will not make people happy."

- **Thomas Stanley**, *Stop Acting Rich*

29

MONTHLY PAYMENTS

Strive to get away from the monthly payment mentality as early in life as possible. The monthly payment mentality? Instead of looking at the issues you should look at (total debt, the interest rate, and the length of loan), you end up fixated on the monthly payment only. Instead of seeing a $30,000 debt at 5% for 7 years, you only see a $288 monthly payment. Don't do that. How?

- **Don't fall for the advertising gimmicks that take your attention away from what you should be focused on and instead highlight your attention on the "low" monthly payment that you want. It's a bad magic trick.**

- **Do focus on everything that is involved with the loan before deciding on whether you can afford it. Just because you can afford a monthly payment doesn't mean you should take out the loan. Keep reminding yourself of that key point.**

Let's take a look at a real-life example to better understand why the monthly payment mentality should be avoided. Let's say you are thinking about buying a Jet Ski to have some fun on the lake. A friend tells you where to go to get a great deal. So, off you go to buy "fun."

When you enter the store, the salesman quickly greets you and starts explaining how wonderful the Jet Skis are and how they have a special sale going on right now. He asks you what you can afford to pay per month and you say $200. He runs some numbers based on your credit score and he comes out with a great deal that will only cost you $195 per month. It sounds good, right? Let's look closer.

I can promise you that Jet Ski will cost you a great deal more than $195. *The total cost might very well end up over $10,000* based on the length of the loan and the interest rate you will pay. P.S. Do not expect the salesman to discuss that big number or the interest rate because he knows that might scare you off and the sale will not happen. Is that $10,000 it? Hell, no. That is simply the beginning.

Those highly trained salesmen will try to sell you a warranty on that Jet Ski as they scare you with stories of people who did not get a warranty. They tell you it is as simple as adding it to the monthly payment (increasing the cost over time because of the interest paid). Will you need a trailer? Probably, what will that cost? Where will you put that Jet Ski? Do you need storage? How much will storage cost you?

What about the yearly cost to run the Jet Ski? Here we could be talking about gas you burn getting to the water, on the water and then going back home. What about the maintenance that will be required each Summer AND Winter? What about insurance? What about any registration costs? How much will that Jet Ski be worth in a year or two (not much thanks to a thing called depreciation)?

When you consider buying that expensive toy, you had best realize just how costly it will be over time. Go into the process with that knowledge BEFORE buying it. You might just realize that renting or borrowing a Jet Ski would be the best option in many situations. This new way of thinking is the beginning of financial wisdom.

"Economists who have studied the relationship between education and economic growth confirm what common sense suggests: The number of college degrees is not nearly as important as how well students develop cognitive skills, such as critical thinking and problem-solving ability."

- **Derek Bok**

30

STUFF

The amount of stuff you buy in your life will tell us a lot about your future financial standing. Why? Stuff loses value and importance very fast, causing you to head to the department store for more stuff. This discussion brings us to the hedonic treadmill, materialism, advertising, and how all those things affect your future.

Here are the basics. *Stuff will not make you happy*. Stuff? All that CRAP that advertisers promote day after day after day. New phones, new computers, new outfits, new cars, new homes, maybe even a new life! The message is pretty clear. Seek happiness through some external source. There is a problem with that approach to finding that wonderful thing called happiness. It doesn't work.

Happiness never has and never will come to those who think the next great external thing is going to make them happier. No matter what that item is, it doesn't hold the clue to more happiness in your life. This brings us to the hedonic treadmill. The hedonic treadmill explains how we adapt to the "great" thing that enters our world. The endorphins raise our level of perceived happiness to a very high level, but quickly, we fall back to where we started. Let's take a look at buying a new vehicle.

It is very natural to feel a burst of what feels like happiness when you drive off the lot with a brand new piece of metal called a car or truck. Here is the problem. In a very short period of time, that new vehicle turns into the used vehicle that doesn't elicit the same feelings as the new vehicle did. You have adapted to the stimulus. Your sense of happiness drops very quickly back to what it was before the new vehicle entered your life.

This feeling can cause you to think you just got the wrong car, which can send you in a different direction to find the "right" car. There is no right car. To understand the hedonic treadmill is to understand this issue of materialism and the world of stuff. When you value stuff over human connections, you end up less satisfied with life. Materialism is something that should be avoided if you want true happiness and financial freedom.

So, why do so many people fall for this time after time? Some exceptionally smart people design advertising campaigns that reach our emotions as they tie their product or service to our drive to be happy, successful, popular, prosperous, etc. They are all lies, but they are very effective lies and that's why we need to arm ourselves with knowledge on the subject as we take control of our money AND our lives.

What can you do about it? As early in your life as possible, reject a materialistic life. Own what you need and maybe a bit extra, but stop yourself from buying more and more and more. You will pay a big price if you don't get a handle on this issue at a young age.

The truth is out there when you are ready to hear it. Stuff has little value to those who seek a better life for themselves and the people they care about. You can learn more on this challenging subject by reading *The High Price of Materialism* by Tim Kasser.

Enlightenment to follow!

"Materialistic values of wealth, status, and image work against close interpersonal relationships and connection to others, two hallmarks of psychological health and high quality of life."

– **Tim Kasser,** *The High Price of Materialism*

31

BIG TICKET PURCHASES

This chapter *can* save you hundreds of thousands of dollars when you apply it to your life. That last statement was not an exaggeration. I recommend reading this chapter many times to fully grasp the overarching message. It is critically important to think through every big ticket purchase you make with your money from this point going forward.

Big ticket purchase? This could be a home, a car, a boat, a patio, a motorcycle, a swimming pool, a new kitchen, a new bathroom, etc. Those items cost a great deal of money and opportunity cost will play a very important role in deciding whether you should buy, wait, or decline that next big purchase.

Example? You are looking to buy a new car because your old car is looking dated and your friends are making fun of you over the lack of technology inside and the faded paint and dents on the outside. You find a great new car at a local dealership that will *only* run you $428 per month, which you could afford to pay. What will it really cost you?

Let's say you buy a $30,200 car on a 6-year loan with a 4.9% interest rate with a $5,000 trade-in on the old car. Your registration cost will go up a lot in the first year and the following years because the car is so expensive. Your insurance goes up a lot every year because now you need full coverage on a more expensive vehicle instead of liability only on the older vehicle.

How much are you out over the next six years? It is not a stretch to say you are out more than $40,000 over the next six years because you wanted a new vehicle instead of the serviceable vehicle you had. Now, let's see what that $40,000 could have done for you elsewhere.

What would you have if you saved $600 per month (you can do this because you are not making that car payment and you are paying rock bottom insurance and registration cost, while maintaining your car with great care) for six years compounded at 8% yearly in a diversified stock index mutual fund? It equals $55,630.12.

That is a difference of **$95,630.12**. At the end of that period, you might consider buying a vehicle because you need it as the maintenance costs start to pile up on your older vehicle OR you might decide to delay the purchase even further as you allow your investments to compound even more over time.

The first approach has you buying a depreciating asset (car) that will lose value in some pretty big ways with high yearly costs (insurance and taxes). The second approach has you buying an appreciating asset (stocks) at a low yearly cost (less than .2% per year in a low-cost index fund). The choice will be yours when that time arrives.

The bigger and more expensive the asset, the more time and deliberation you should put into whether it is a wise decision to buy. The key is to think long-term (increasing your net worth) instead of short-term (what is my monthly payment).

Weighing the opportunity cost (where your money is working best for you) *will help you make better financial decisions.* To say this is important, is an extreme understatement. Decision after decision will tell us where you end up financially. Make the right decision.

"From experience, I can tell you that it is very difficult to unlearn something you have always known. We tend to cling to old, familiar, and comfortable ways of thinking in unreasonable ways. Change is difficult and painful. We resist it. We rationalize our aversion to it. We fight for the old ideas every step of the way. We practically have to be hit over the head with a better idea before we will consider it."

- **Frank Armstrong III**, *The Informed Investor*

32

THE 50/50 RULE

If you learn to live by the 50/50 rule, financial freedom will find its way to your door step sooner rather than later. This is all about the process of living below your means so one day you can live without a job. What is the 50/50 rule? You live on 50% of your gross pay (before anything is taken out) after allocating the other 50% for taxes and savings. Let's take a look at how this can work.

Let's say you earn a $36,000 salary per year. You would cut that amount up in half as you plan your future going forward. You would take $18,000 to live on and the other $18,000 would be used to pay taxes and save into your emergency account, retirement plan at work, Roth IRA and/or pay extra on your debts. Let's start with the $18,000 that will be used for your living expenses.

You can spend $1,500 per month on anything you like, but keep in mind, it must cover your bills as well as your fun. You would be wise to start tracking your spending and budgeting carefully so the money does not run out before the month does. You can learn more on this subject by going to thecrazymaninthepinkwig.com and hit on the *tracking your spending* link under the menu. More on that, later in the book.

The other $1,500 must cover taxes and savings. Let's start with 30% going to taxes. In 2017, you will pay 7.65% in FICA tax on every dollar you earn (this goes to Social Security and Medicare). You will also pay federal income tax. Let's assume you have about 15% withheld from your paycheck (this will vary based on your withholding number you selected when turning in your W-4). Next up, state income tax. Most people pay that as well. Let's add in 7.35% for state (this varies by state).

The remaining 20% is for savings. How you allocate those savings is up to you. If you have a great deal of debt, you might consider putting most of it toward that, using the *debt avalanche* or *debt snowball* methods that are discussed later in the book. Take some time to consider opportunity cost before deciding on one of those issues or investing the money elsewhere at work or in a Roth IRA at Vanguard.

Let's say your debt is minimal and/or your interest rates are very low so you decide on placing your contributions elsewhere. Getting your emergency savings up to at least $1,000 would be wise. Higher could be warranted with a family and other responsibilities. Once that is taken care of, investing in your company retirement plan and Roth IRA are no-brainers for those who want to create wealth over time.

Let's assume you are going to save the entire 20% into retirement accounts. You might put 10% into a 401(k) plan at work and the other 10% into a Roth IRA at a place like Vanguard as you set up automatic payments each month out of your paycheck and/or bank account. Invest wisely when doing this and that means focusing on inexpensive index funds. That will be explained in more detail later in the book as well.

BOOM, you drop the mic and walk off the stage knowing your money will be making you money. *Compound interest is one amazing thing.* Identify your plan and implement it, placing your finances on auto-pilot, while you enjoy your life. You live by the 50/50 rule (no matter what your income) month after month, year after year, and decade after decade. Financial freedom to follow.

"Success is not a destination, but the road that you're on. Being successful means that you're working hard and walking your walk every day. You can only live your dream by working hard towards it. That's living your dream."

- **Marlon Wayans**

33

RETIREMENT PLANS

Many of you will be offered some type of company retirement plan at your workplace. You want to jump on this opportunity as soon as possible. These plans are one of the best ways to build wealth over time. I call them *freedom plans*. Here are the basics.

If you are one of the few who are offered a pension, count your blessings. They are gradually going away. A pension? The official name is a defined benefit plan. The employer usually puts in most if not all of the money. These types of plans are really good deals, but they are expensive for the employer, which is why they are going away.

The program that replaced pensions is called a defined contribution plan. These plans have numbers or letters attached to them like 401(k), 403(b), 457, and TSP (see the glossary for more information). The key is identifying what is offered to you and then making wise choices with your future investments. There are thousands of dollars at stake. Get informed!

You may be offered a Traditional (pre-tax) and Roth (after tax) retirement plan at work. Which one should you choose? The answer is relatively straightforward once you understand your current tax situation and your gross income. Saying that, it will require you to estimate, as best you can, your future taxes and income levels. Let's take a look.

Here is a rule of thumb you *could* consider using when considering your current income and tax brackets. If you make under $60,000 a year, go with the Roth. If you make over that amount, go with the Traditional. If your total family income is under $100,000, go with the Roth. If your family income is over $100,000, go with the Traditional.

Of course, each situation is different based on what state you live in and the income tax or lack thereof in that state at that time. Don't lose too much sleep over the matter. Figure out which one (Traditional or Roth) you think is best at that time and go with that. *You can always change it later if your income and/or tax situation changes.*

How much? ALWAYS invest up to the matching amount, no matter whether it is dollar for dollar or 50 cents on the dollar. Get that FREE money and while you're at it, identify your vesting period (how long before that matching money belongs to YOU). Invest more as best you can, but also consider your investment options within the plan.

Investment options? The funds your company provides you are all quite different and sadly, expensive in many cases. Look for low cost index funds when starting out or target date funds with costs below .2% (the expense ratio). Costs make a HUGE difference over time. Learn more on that issue by reading *What Color is the Sky*.

Don't get cute. Owning one inexpensive Total Stock Market Index Fund or one Target Date Retirement Fund with a big number like 2050 is all you need to get started. The bigger the number, the more stocks you will own, the more risk you will incur, and the expected higher returns should follow over time. Now let's cover what you SHOULD NOT do.

DO NOT trade stocks. DO NOT borrow against it. DO NOT listen to the guy in the breakroom who tells you how to time the market. DO NOT put it in a "safe" fund (inflation will eat it up). Finally, DO NOT leave it there when you depart. Move the funds to a Traditional IRA or Roth IRA at Vanguard (more on that later in the book). Take control!

"There is something in people; you might even call it a little bit of a gambling instinct... I tell people investing should be dull. It shouldn't be exciting. Investing should be more like watching paint dry or watching grass grow. If you want excitement, take $800 and go to Las Vegas."

- **Paul Samuleson**, Nobel Laureate in Economics

34

THE ROTH IRA

It is wise to start a Roth IRA soon after getting your diploma. Why? This type of account can be used for many things. And that is a good thing when you are entering an unknown world with unidentified events that will be happening either as expected or, in many cases, unexpected.

What is a Roth IRA? It is a tax-sheltered account that you can use for multiple purposes. It can be used as a retirement account. It can be used as a down payment account for a home purchase. It can also be used as an emergency account. Roth IRAs have turned into hybrid accounts that can serve you in many ways. Go get one!

Where? Go to Vanguard.com and open one with as little as $1,000 (systematically save money into your bank account as needed to reach that minimum amount). Why Vanguard? They offer low cost index funds that grow your account over time. With $1,000 you can start with a Target Retirement Fund that owns stocks and bonds all over the world.

The number that goes with a Target Retirement Fund is important. A 2050 fund will own more stocks in the United States and Overseas than a 2030 fund and therefore it will be riskier and more volatile which *should* produce higher returns over time. If you have $3,000, you can select one of the individual index funds.

One good example for short-term needs would be the Short-Term Bond Index Fund. This low risk fund would be good to own with money you need in the next year or two. A longer-term need might have you investing in the Total Stock Market Index Fund, which owns all the businesses that make up the U.S. economy. Can you say awesome?!!!!

There are rules that go with a Roth IRA so be sure to understand them before investing. Here are the basics. Your earned income (money from your job) must equal or surpass your contribution amount (you must earn $4,000 to invest $4,000). You can only put in a limited amount each year ($5,500 for 2017 when you are under age 50). The withdrawal rules can be a bit challenging so pay special attention to the next few points.

You can pull any of your Roth IRA *contributions* out any time you like without paying a penalty or taxes. You will pay a penalty and taxes if you pull the *earnings* out prior to age 59.5. There are exceptions. If your earnings are qualified (your Roth IRA is 5 years old) you can pull out $10,000 in earnings for the down payment on a first-time home purchase without penalty and without taxes being owed.

A couple who is consistent with their contributions over a 5-year period could save up a nice chunk of money into each account as they plan for their future needs. This will allow them to move into a home with other money (emergency account) set aside for the inevitable expenses they never saw coming. And, trust me, they will come.

The Roth IRA could be your ticket to a brighter future if used wisely and that means understanding the rules in detail prior to contributing and certainly prior to withdrawing any funds. *Inform yourself carefully as you make smart decisions every step of the way.* More information on becoming the wise investor will follow in later chapters.

"We should design a life for ourselves where we can spend our days doing what we love. To that end, we should save every penny we can early in our adult life, so we quickly buy ourselves some financial freedom. In our 40s or 50s, we might use that freedom to switch into a career that's perhaps less lucrative, but which we may find more fulfilling."

- **Jonathan Clements**, *How to Think About Money*

35

SPENDING PART I

How you handle your spending after getting that lovely diploma is a BIG DEAL. The recommendations you see below should be used as a guide as you traverse through life with the money you earn and ultimately spend. Where you end up in your future will have a great deal to do with how you spend your money TODAY.

Step #1 is tracking your spending. Immediately, start a system where you track every dollar you spend. How? Identify one method of payment that works for you and then stay consistent with that method over long periods of time. Method? Use either cash, a debit card, or a credit card to make all your purchases so it is easy to track.

Which method is best? *The method you will stick with through good times and bad.* You will generally find this easier when using a debit or credit card, rather than cash. Why? You have a statement at the end of each month and you can sign on whenever you like to see exactly where your spending has taken place.

The key is to use one method only so there is less hassle or possible mistakes. Mistakes? Using multiple cards and cash gets complicated and it is very easy to lose track of your spending because there are too many places to look. You want to create a simple and sustainable approach to tracking your spending.

I am not against using cash only to track your expenses, but I just don't think most people will stay with it over long periods of time. If you do want to use cash only, bring a pad and pen with you wherever you go so you can write down every dollar you spend.

Let's say you have decided to use a debit card. Pay for everything that you possibly can with that one card and avoid using other cards or cash so you have a clear understanding on where the money went. Next, print off that statement at the end of the month and start adding up the amounts into their respective categories.

Categories? They might include groceries, the cable bill, internet service, phone, entertainment, eating out, mortgage/rent, insurance, gifting, travel, clothing, utilities, gas, and whatever else you spend money on. The more specific you are, the better (breaking up your grocery bill into drinks, meat and other food is one example).

Next, put the numbers down on paper or in a spreadsheet and see where your money is going on a monthly basis. This process helps you evaluate whether your money is going to the right places. If so, continue on with what you are doing with your spending. If not, change course, and start spending your money differently.

This process *should* take no more than 10 minutes a month. You can go to thecrazymaninthepinkwig.com and download a free spreadsheet under the *tracking your spending* link. The formulas are built in to help you with the addition and subtraction and it's all FREE. You can also use mint.com or powerwallet.com if you like. They are FREE as well.

"If you're a young person starting out and you see someone with the latest expensive toys, think about how they might have acquired them. Too many of those items were probably bought on credit—with sleepless nights as a complementary accessory. Many of those people will never truly be rich. Instead, they will be stressed."

- **Andrew Hallam**, *Millionaire Teacher*

36

SPENDING PART II

It's time to decide what you need and what you don't. You can't have it all and don't listen to people who tell you such nonsense. You must make decisions on your spending based on your priorities. *Identify what is important to you and let go of what is not.* That is how you start to take control of your financial life.

Step #2 deals with setting up a budget to make sure your money is allocated properly based on your goals for the future. A budget? You identify very specific amounts of money that you allow yourself to spend on each category. Each dollar should be earmarked properly after you track your spending for at least two months.

Does everyone need a budget? The truth is, no, not everyone does. Why? Some people are "tight" with their money. They spend only when they have to and waste is not in their vocabulary. If you are one of those people, budgeting is probably not that big of a deal. Tracking your spending will probably suffice. As for the rest of you, put together a budget.

Budgeting provides structure to a financial life. It gives those who are not so organized a clear-cut amount per item to focus on per month. As a good rule of thumb, every person should start a budget soon after earning money. Then, see where that goes over time based on how their situation changes from one year to the next.

Here is an example. You have been tracking your spending for three months and identified that you spend $120 per month eating out at restaurants. You decide that is too much and give yourself a budget of $60 per month, taking the other $60 and paying extra on your debt.

You are using a debit card every time you go out to eat and you decide to add up your eating out costs each week to keep close track of that $60 limit. After week three, you see that you have spent $58 eating out. What then? You don't allow yourself to eat out for the rest of the month if you are going to go over $60. You STOP eating out.

When the month is over, your $60 limit kicks in again and that's when you give yourself permission to eat out with friends at restaurants around the city. What happens if your friends try to talk you into breaking your budget? They are not very good friends if they are trying to convince you to do something that is not in your best interest.

People you want to be around, support your goals, they don't put you down. Surround yourself with the right people and your budget and your life can work quite nicely. Surround yourself with the wrong people and your budget and your life could get blown the hell up!

After a few months, you might not have to monitor your statements so carefully as you start to develop the right habits to keep you honest with the budget month after month. This will allow you to pay down debt and save more money for your future needs. Winner, winner, chicken dinner!

"To make the smart changes you're looking for, you first need to learn the rules of the financial road. ... The rules are the same for men and women, singles and marrieds, the young and the old. ... Clarity helps create trust, in yourself and each other. That leads you to a better place."

- **Jane Bryant Quinn**, *Smart and Simple Financial Strategies for Busy People*

37

SPENDING PART III

You MUST learn to control your weak spot if you ever hope to get ahead in life with your finances. What is the weak spot? That is the area in your life where you overspend on something that is of great importance to you. This could include vehicles, shoes, clothing, purses, computers, travel, food, phones, decorating, guns, and even those little angels we call children.

Once you start tracking your spending, you will quickly identify where the money is going and in many cases, too much is going to a few specific items. The weak spot(s) become very clear at that point. Budgeting for the weak spot(s) can make a world of difference as you look to improve your financial picture.

So, what are your weak spots? Be brutally honest with that person in the mirror. Don't beat yourself up about the issue, just be honest. Let's pick on the ladies for the moment. Let's say one woman has a weak spot for shoes. She identifies how much she has spent on them for the past year and that number comes to $1,200.

She is stunned by that number and decides to budget $30 a month, which translates to $360 a year for that weak spot in her financial life. Why? Paying down debt and increasing her financial freedom is more important than having boxes of shoes in the back of the closet that will be worn once or twice before being relegated back to their resting place in the box.

What happens if she sees some shoes she loves and they cost $180? She can buy them if she chooses to, as long as it does not take her over the $360 maximum for the year, but that takes care of six months of the shoe budget. Those shoes better be pretty damn amazing!

There is another method that will help you with that weak spot. *Avoid impulse buying*. You can do this by waiting 30 days before buying something that you think you need. Many times, after the 30-day waiting period is up, you have forgotten what it was that you wanted. And might remind you just how many purchases end up being pure impulse.

One final method when dealing with a weak spot is to pay with cash when buying something you love. For many, it can be much more difficult to pay cash for the weak spot than to plunk down a card (debit or credit). Cash has a way of feeling much more real causing you to question the purchase and what it will do to your bank account.

Getting your spending under control is a HUGE issue. Many financial problems stem from people overspending. In some cases, people overspend because of the problems in their life. They cope by shopping. Find other ways to deal with the stresses in life like going for a walk, sitting down with a friend over lunch or possibly meditating.

It's all about doing what is necessary to get yourself a plan that will put you in a better place financially AND psychologically. Remember, a plan provides direction. Winging it causes a mess. Get yourself a plan. Stick to it every month. And be sure to make it as simple and sustainable as possible. Your future self will thank you one day.

"Academic researchers and mental health experts agree that for some people, spending money does for them what abusing food, drugs, or alcohol does for others. Compulsive spenders who invest a damaging amount of time and financial resources into shopping typically suffer from anxiety disorders, depression, and low self-esteem. Compulsive shoppers get a high from shopping and spending. These feelings of euphoria provide a distraction from and help buy (at least while they're shopping) negative feelings about themselves and their lives."

- **Eric Tyson**, *Let's Get Real About Money*

38

CREDIT PART I

Credit is not good, nor is it bad. The key is to understand how to use it in a smart way. Using credit wisely is simply a way of dealing with financial matters in a responsible way that *can* save you THOUSANDS of dollars over time. Let's start with a few basics.

Go to annualcreditreport.com to view your 3 *credit reports* for free each year (review one report every 4 months for simplicity). Spend a little time making sure everything on those three reports is correct. If you find something wrong, notify the credit bureau and get it taken off. Those credit reports are important!

If you have a credit card, pay it off in full every month come hell or high water. If you cannot do that, you are not ready to have a credit card. The proper use of credit can help you get your finances organized. If your life is chaotic and your finances are a mess and you have a hard time remembering when bills come due, don't get a credit card.

Some people can handle credit with no problem. Others become credit addicts and if you happen to be one of them, watch yourself! It's kind of like alcohol. Some people can have a few drinks and call it quits. Others cannot handle alcohol and so they should stay away from consuming any drinks. Credit is no different.

Get your FICO score to 760 (ranges from 300 to 850). Why? It will get you the lowest possible interest rate when you take out a loan for a house, a car (not required, but worth considering based on the interest rate), or something else (a business loan for example). Don't waste your time trying to go much above 760. The interest rate will not get better.

How do you get that score to 760? (1) Pay your bills on time (this means getting organized). (2) Use a small amount of credit (under 10%) in relation to what is offered to you (more on those issues in the following chapter). Get those two big pieces squared away and you are well on your way toward increasing your credit score.

If you are having problems getting credit, try these two tips to get you up and running. (1) Have your parents or someone who really trusts you put you on their credit card as an authorized user with the clear understanding that *you will not have a credit card.* This approach works if they have good credit. If so, this will get you started. If they have bad credit, don't do this. You will end up with their bad credit.

(2) Get a secured credit card as you plunk down a few hundred dollars at your local credit union. The lender will put the money into an interest-bearing savings account in your name (it will be locked up, but still yours). In turn they will give you a credit limit on a credit card for that amount. After 6 months or so, ask to have the secured card dropped and you will have yourself a regular credit card.

Track your three *credit scores* from the big three bureaus at creditkarma.com (TransUnion and Equifax) and credit.com (Experian). Both sites are free. Ignore the onslaught of advertising and monitor your status there at no cost. Increase your score gradually by focusing on the big two items I mentioned earlier and the other three methods (age of credit, types of credit, and inquiries) that have a lesser affect. With a bit of patience and due diligence, you can reach a FICO score of 760.

"Lower credit scores mean you pay more in interest for your car loan, home mortgage, and credit cards. Low credit scores could cause you to be turned down for the credit you deserve, be denied insurance, or even be forced to pay higher insurance premiums."

- **Stephen Snyder,** *Do You Make These 38 Mistakes With Your Credit?*

39

CREDIT PART II

Let's spend some time talking about credit cards. Are they evil? No, they are pieces of plastic. Plastic cannot be evil. It has no pulse. *What makes credit cards good or bad is the person who is using them.* It is vital to get that key point down before moving forward.

So, should you have a credit card? If you know how to handle a credit card, they can be convenient. How to handle one? You need to be organized so you know when the statement comes in and when the bill is due. You need to pay it off in full every month. If you can't say yes to either of those two things, stay away from credit cards. If you can, keep reading.

Get yourself two credit cards that are taken in most establishments. This means a Visa or a MasterCard. Why two? You want a primary card and a backup in case something happens to the primary AND the second one will help you with the whole credit utilization thing, which I will discuss later in this chapter.

Get two cards that pay you back in cash with every purchase. Here are two: [Chase Freedom](#) and [Citi Double Cash Back](#). Every time you use the cards, you will get some cash back. That is FREE money and it can be yours if you are smart with the use of the credit cards. Just don't go hog wild. Only use the credit card if you would normally pay cash for the item.

Enjoy the perks and there are many. You will get liability protection (if someone steals your card and uses it, in most cases, you are out no money as long as you report it within 30 days). You will get purchase, price, return and extended warranty protection. You also can get the rebate. And here is the kicker. It's all FREE.

If you cannot get one of those cards yet because of your lack of credit, go get that secured credit card. Just don't go overboard on the amount of credit cards you end up acquiring. Two will do just fine. Store credit cards are not needed so just say no thank you when the clerk pushes them on you with the discount enticement. Here is how you use credit cards to increase your credit score.

(1) Pay your credit cards off at the same time each month. You can tell the credit card companies when you want the bill to come due. This process is all about getting organized so you don't make the mistake of missing a payment or being late for one. Both of those blunders will cost you dearly and MUST be avoided at all costs.

(2) Increase your credit limits as high as the credit card issuer will let you. No, that doesn't mean you max out the cards. It means you want to use less than 10% of your available credit. For example, if you have a $1,000 credit limit and you have an average balance of $500 per month, you are using 50%. That's not good. You want to get that number under 10%.

Call up your credit card company and request a credit limit to $5,000 for instance. If you get it, and use your credit card as usual, the $500 per month balance ends up being 10% instead of 50%. That will increase your credit score quickly.

Consider increasing the limit on both credit cards to high numbers ($20,000 per card will do) and then use the card to pay the bills, keeping the usage under 10%. Credit cards can work very nicely for those who know how to use them. Be that type of person.

"I haven't reported my missing credit card to the police because whoever stole it is spending less than my wife."
                                                    - Ilie Nastase

40

CREDIT PART III

Increasing your credit score (FICO score) can save you thousands and thousands of dollars over time as you buy homes, cars, businesses, and other items with a loan. It's worth your trouble to get that credit score up and over 760. It simply comes down to handling it in a smart way.

As stated earlier, (1) pay your bills on time and (2) use 10% or less of your available credit on those credit cards. Once you accomplish those two feats, it's time to deal with the issue in other ways that have a lesser impact on your score, but are still important.

(3) Avoid derogatory comments. They do nothing but hurt you. If you have them, find ways to get them off your credit report by contacting who it was that put them there. Take the initiative to fix your credit report where you can.

(4) Improve the age of each individual line of credit. This means you don't drop credit cards unless you have a good reason (which also includes not being dropped from mom and dad's credit card). It will take a bit of time to improve this for those of you who are just starting out.

(5) The type of credit (car loan, home loan, credit card, etc.) has a smaller impact on your score, but it is worth understanding. Lenders like to see various types of loans on your account from other institutions. With that being said, I would not take out any loans that you don't need.

(6) Keep your credit inquiries by a business or lender to a minimum by requesting credit only when needed. Hard inquiries by a business or lender can reduce your credit score. Keep those inquiries to a minimum.

Be patient with this process. A high credit score takes a bit of time and effort. The credit scores you see at creditkarma.com and credit.com are not your FICO score, but they are close. P.S. Checking those sites will not constitute a hard inquiry. Do it as often as you like.

The #1 reason to get a high credit score is to get a low interest rate on a mortgage when buying a home. A high credit score *could* save $50,000 or more in interest based on the size and length of the loan. Think about that for a minute. Is it worth it to get a credit score of 760? Hell, yes!

The other types of loans are less important in comparison based on the size of the loan (a $20,000 loan vs. a $200,000 mortgage for example). The time you put in now will pay you back many times over as your future plays out. Keep reminding yourself of that key fact.

Sit down with your spouse and do this together if you are married. When you take out a joint loan, both credit scores will matter a great deal as the lender brings them together to form one score. Allow me to state the obvious; you want two high scores.

NEVER go see a lender to get a loan without knowing your credit score. You should have just as much information as the lender when you make the request to borrow money. You can do that and you should do that. Take charge of YOUR credit.

"I don't use a debit card. The safest thing is a credit card because you're using the bank's money. If someone accesses your information, they are stealing the bank's money, not yours."

- **Frank Abagnale,** *Catch Me If You Can*

41

DEBT PART I

Should you take on debt? Maybe and maybe not is the answer to that difficult question that cannot be answered easily with a yes or a no. Be careful when people tell you debt is bad or debt is good. Debt can be bad, but it also can be needed for a temporary period until you can get yourself in a better situation financially. Let's explore the many nuances that come with this issue. First, the bad stuff.

When is debt bad? When you borrow money to buy depreciating assets that go down in value over time, it's usually bad. Two specific debts that far too many people have would include credit card debt and vehicle debt. Always avoid the credit card debt and limit your vehicle loans as best you can by saving up for your next vehicle purchase.

When is debt really bad? Any time you take out a loan from someone other than a bank or credit union, it's usually really bad debt. The interest rates will be high and there is a reason the bank or credit union doesn't want to give you a loan. Payday lenders should be avoided like the plaque. Businesses that rent out furniture and technology are no go's as well. They are stealing from you in a legal way.

What about loans against your retirement plan at work? Hell, no! You are stealing from your future. Do not see that retirement plan as anything, but a long-term investment that you feed month after month while you are working. So, one day you can use that money to escape the world of work. Others may borrow against their retirement plan, but don't let that happen to you. It is a really bad idea.

What about the needed debt (called good debt by some people)? A college loan will be needed if you don't have the cash to go to college and you are ready to go. A car loan will be needed if you need a car to get to work and you don't have the cash to buy one. A home loan will be needed if you don't have the cash for that large purchase. Finally, a business loan will be needed if you want to start a business and you need start-up capital.

There is a catch with all those loans. While you can make a case for all four of those options, that doesn't mean you should pull the trigger and accept them. You can end up in bankruptcy court with college loans, car loans, home loans and business loans.

Those loans do not equal future success so keep that in mind. They *can* be used temporarily to get yourself in a better positon going forward with your life. Take those loans out with great care and a clear understanding of just how much debt you are assuming.

Just because a lender wants to give you a loan doesn't mean you should take it. Keep saying that to yourself until it sinks in. Whether it is the federal government with student loans or your local bank or credit union, you can turn them down. You can say no thanks.

You can take out less money than you qualify for on whatever loan you are considering. Make sure you are making these important decisions and not the lender. You will be the one who must pay the money back with interest. Minimize your debt. Freedom to follow.

"All of us college students are racking up these bills. There is this massive amount of pressure that is slowly just building up, waiting, and it's fixing to collapse all on us."

- **Student with $22,000 in student loans,** *Broke, Busted and Disgusted*

42

DEBT PART II

What does a person do when they have a big pile of debt? Worry is probably near the top of many people's list. And you have a right to worry. *That debt can feel like you are carrying an elephant on your back.* It is imperative that you identify a very specific plan when considering how you are going to pay it off. These questions should be answered first.

- **What type of debt is it (student, car, credit card, etc.)?**

- **What is the total amount you owe on each loan?**

- **What is the interest rate on each loan?**

- **What is the minimum monthly payment on each loan?**

Once you have identified those answers, it is time to design a plan to pay those loans off. Consider the debt avalanche or the debt snowball (explained in more detail in the chapters to follow). Both can work, pick the one that works best for you and then DO IT.

This is the time where the issue of opportunity cost comes into play once again. Opportunity cost forces you to consider where each dollar you have should go based on what it can do for you. Here is where I would like you to pick what I call an anchor.

Select an interest rate (4% for example) that you would use to decide whether to *pay extra on debt* (loans with rates higher than 4%) vs. *paying nothing extra* (loans with rates below 4%) and putting the extra money toward low cost stock index mutual funds.

This approach implies that you know how to invest wisely. Do you? If not, get smarter on the subject by reading *The Little Book of Common Sense Investing* by John Bogle and *The Smartest Investment Book You'll Ever Read* by Daniel Solin. There will be more information on investing later in the book.

There are many variables you will want to consider as you anticipate your options on paying down debt vs. investing in your future. Your future is a big question mark right now. How you deal with the debt in your life is a big deal. Answer the questions below prior to moving forward.

- **If you are married, what is your spouse's debt situation?**

- **Do you have an emergency fund? If so, how much is in it?**

- **Are you just getting by with your income? Where can you cut?**

- **Do you have a retirement plan with a match? How much?**

Here is the bottom line for those who have a ton of debt. Don't wait for some miracle to happen. Make your own miracle. Now is the time to identify a plan to pay off your debt while still building wealth in your retirement plans at work and outside of work. Make it happen.

"Because of my age, I am older than most of the students in my class and I've actually spent a lot of time in the real world and at present, I am a Junior and I have so far learned absolutely nothing that has applied to my real life in the real world, ever."

- **Student with $45,000 in student loans,** *Broke, Busted and Disgusted*

43

DEBT PART III

When deciding whether to take on debt, what should you consider? A lot is the short answer. Take your time to explore the issue carefully because the decision on whether to take out debt will pop up again and again in the future. Every decision will have lasting consequences.

What are the right decisions? The only good reason to take on debt is because it will help you in your future. If a loan won't improve your future life, don't take it out. If you're not sure if it will help you, wait until you have more evidence that makes it a good decision (or not). Let's look at three debt examples that will apply to many people.

Should you take out a mortgage to buy a house? Do you plan to live there for many years? Can you afford the 20% down payment on the home? Can you afford to pay about 10% a year in taxes, insurance, interest on the loan, maintenance, and the inevitable upgrades to improve the home? Is your job secure? Is your relationship solid?

Should you take out a car loan? Do you have a car now? If yes, why do you need to replace it? If no, what is the reason to buy a car? How much are you willing to pay? Are you buying a new car or a used car? How long do you intend to keep it? Do you need an extended warranty? Can you afford the registration and insurance costs on the new purchase?

Should you take out student loans for college? Where should you go? Should the debt be federal loans or private loans? Does it matter if they are fixed rates or adjustable rates? What will the degree get you? What kind of pay does that degree usually get a person? How much will it cost to get that degree? What is the amount of money you will need to borrow?

If any of that scared you, I don't blame you. It would scare the hell out of me as a high school or college graduate. It probably explains one reason on why I chose the military right out of high school. That is a place you can go without going into deep debt. The answers were more clear cut there and much less clear in the "civilian" world.

It is important that you ask those many questions long before you take out one of those loans (or not). Some loans you may decide are worth it because you see how it will help you in the future. On the other hand, you may decide to decline other loans because you don't see how the loans will benefit you long-term.

Debt *can* be used as leverage to catapult you into a better financial position in the future. *It can also bankrupt you and leave you feeling bitter and destroyed.* The time to think through these issues carefully is BEFORE taking out the debt, not after the fact, when the damage has been done and you have signed on the dotted line.

Here is the bottom line. Debt *might* be a necessary evil at certain times in your life based on your unique situation. At other times, debt will not be needed and you should avoid it and the stress that comes with it. Your ability to identify when and when not to take out debt will end up telling us a great deal about your future. Make the right call.

"I've done the math; it's not going to look very good. …I hadn't really looked at the backend of what that really meant."

- **Graduate with $140,000 in student loans,** *Broke, Busted and Disgusted*

44

STUDENT LOANS PART I

This chapter addresses the issue of whether you should take out student loans and what is smart when you do. These are two separate issues and they will be discussed individually. This chapter speaks to the high school graduate who is contemplating student loans and whether they are worth it. The next two chapters speaks to the college graduate who is leaving school with student loans and what to do with them.

You don't need to take out student loans. There are thousands of high school graduates who never take out student loans. How? (1) They get scholarships and grants to cover the cost. (2) They join the military and the government pays for college. (3) They and/or their parents have saved the needed funds prior to attending. (4) They work their way through school and pay only what their salary allows. (5) They don't go to college.

There are many other reasons, but those five items will be the focus of this chapter. How many of those options are available to you? For many Americans, all five items *may* apply in one way or another. There are many ways to pick up an education beyond high school without taking on student loan debt. You need to know that as you enter a world that entices you into taking on tons of debt.

Now, I know some of you might be shaking your head, thinking that I don't understand YOUR situation. You are right, I don't. But here is what I do know. Taking on student loan debt is a choice. Only take it out when all other options have been eliminated. Piling up a big amount of student loans can make life much more difficult, limiting your opportunities in life because you are stuck with so much debt.

If you need student loans, take out as little as you possibly can and that means only federal loans that are *subsidized* (interest accrues on the loan starting six months after school ends) and *unsubsidized* (interest accrues on the loan immediately). Avoid private loans whenever possible.

DO NOT take out student loan debt for anything beyond school tuition. If you need that money for living expenses, rethink your plan. If you need that money for spring break or any other fun activity, check yourself in the mirror. Don't be that person.

DO NOT take out any student loan debt if you don't know what you want to do. Don't spend 6 or 7 years "finding yourself," while picking up more and more debt as you switch from one major to another. Figure that out as best you can before taking out a loan.

DO NOT go to college to party. It will be fun for a few months and then you will pay for that fun for decades to come. That's just dumb. Go to college to learn, to think critically and to grow as a human being. If you aren't ready to do that, wait until you are.

PAY CASH to a community college before taking out a loan to a university. If you can get your first two years paid for with cash instead of a loan, do it. The education will be similar and the reduced stress of having less debt will be worth it.

This is a BUSINESS DECISION that needs to be made with a mature mind and a hand on your wallet. Pause before taking out student loans. If you cannot see how a student loan will pay off for you in the future, wait until you do. Less debt equals more freedom.

"I think it was too easy to borrow money for school. On top of my loans, my parents have loans on my education."

- **Student with $45,000 in student loans,** *Broke, Busted and Disgusted*

45

STUDENT LOANS PART II

This chapter deals with the student leaving college with student loans and they land a decent job that will allow them to have choices on how they will pay off their student loan debt. Here are some questions to contemplate as you leave a college campus with a diploma.

- **What is the total amount that you owe?**
- **What approach should you use to pay them off?**
- **Should you pay the minimum?**
- **Should you implement the debt snowball?**
- **Should you select the debt avalanche instead?**
- **How long will it take you to pay those loans off?**
- **Will you have any fun in the meantime?**

Those are all valid questions and they need good answers. Now is the time to understand your options so you can make an informed decision. As we address the issue, always consider that thing called opportunity cost with each decision you make.

One dollar going one place cannot go somewhere else. Taking $20 and putting it in a savings account earning .2% would not be wise if you could have taken that $20 and put it down on debt at 6.8%. Any place you put extra savings should be the place where it can do you the most good.

Let's start with the ideal situation. The college graduate gets a nice job with a paycheck that easily covers the student loan payments. Should that person pay extra? You *could* reduce the length of the loans by paying extra on top of the minimum payments. The question is, "Should you?"

Option #1 is to pay off your federal loans over a *10-year period* which is the standard payment plan that the borrower receives. You could take 10 years to pay the loans off, but you will end up paying a whole lot of interest over those 10 years. You would be wise to select one of the two other methods below when possible. P.S. You could also use some combination of the two methods.

Option #2 is the *debt snowball*. Identify your loans by size. Then, pay the smallest loan off first with extra cash no matter what the interest rate, while making minimum payments on the others. Once that small loan is paid off, proceed to the next smallest loan and do the same thing until you end up paying them all off. This method has worked for many based on seeing an entire debt go away.

Option #3 is the *debt avalanche*. Identify your loans by interest rate. You pay extra on the loan with the highest interest rate, while making minimum payments on the others. Once that first loan is paid off, go to the loan with the next highest interest rate. Proceed on until all of loans are paid off. If you stick with it, the debt avalanche is by far the best method financially. You will end up paying less interest over time.

Both approaches can work. The key is to pick the one you will sustain over long periods of time and that requires a bit of introspection. Educate yourself further on this very important subject by going to thecrazymaninthepinkwig.com and hitting on the link *debt management* on the menu screen. It's time to take control!

"It's kind of scary to me to know I have a house payment to pay after I graduate... I have a little bit of fear that I won't be able to pay it off or it will hinder me from doing something that I really want to do."

- **Student with $42,000 in student loans,** *Broke, Busted and Disgusted*

46

STUDENT LOANS PART III

This chapter deals with the student leaving college with student loans and no job or a job that barely pays the bills. If that is you, don't lose hope. There is a way out of this mess, but it won't be easy and it will probably take quite a bit of time. Meet this issue head on and one day, you might just find yourself debt free.

Let's look at the college graduate who makes just enough money from one or more jobs to pay the 10-year loan monthly payment. It will be tempting to sign up for the *income-based repayment plan* on federal loans (there are very specific rules you must meet). It will reduce your payment and give you more money each month for fun. Should you do it?

This will reduce your payment, but you will end up paying more interest over time until the loan is written off at 20 or 25 years based on when you received the federal loans. Do you really want to stretch out the loan that far? I would cut corners where necessary with your monthly budget and pay it off in 10 years if possible.

Less debt will equal more freedom. Letting that debt hang around for decades could very easily limit what you want to do with your life. It could delay marriage. It could delay or eliminate the possibility of buying a home. It could put your life on hold. Let's face it, having school loans still on the books into your 50s and 60s is depressing.

What about the person who has a hard time finding a job? You can try for *loan deferment* where the payment and interest is put on hold. If that is not possible, *loan forbearance* is an option where the payment might be deferred, but the interest piles up. Neither option is good.

DO NOT ignore the loan servicer if you are having problems covering your monthly payment. Contact them immediately and explain your issues as clearly as you can and then see what can be done on their end to make the situation more manageable. Also, the loan servicer can make mistakes and often times they do. Monitor your account carefully!

You took the loans; it is your responsibility to pay them back. Buck up and get it done. You are growing into a mature adult and that means you pay your debts. Do what you must under the circumstances. Moving back in with mom and dad and getting another job would be two options worth considering, agonizing as that may sound.

Everything I just discussed deals with federal student loans. If you have private student loans, the problems can get worse. Many of those loans are adjustable and that means the interest rate can go up, up and away. If there are problems paying, you must negotiate with them and they will probably not be as understanding as the federal government.

There are programs out there created to help those in need and the military can help as well. Educate yourself fully on your many options at student.ed.gov. If you find this chapter a bit depressing, join the club. I have a great deal of sympathy for those of you with big student loans. If you have them, do your best. If you don't, keep it that way!

"Don't borrow more for college than you expect to earn the

first year out of school."

- **Jean Chatzky**, *Money Rules*

47

SAVING PART I

You should save money from each paycheck you make. I am betting some of you have heard that before. The big question is, "Why?" If you can answer that question with a clear and precise answer, you are well on your way toward becoming a financially successful person who saves money consistently over time. Let's look at how it can be done.

Saving money just to save money is not going to work for many people. You need something to save for if you want a savings habit to stick over time. Here is the answer to becoming a great saver: Identify the right goals and your behaviors and habits will fall in line to achieve those goals. *You will become a saver once you have the right goals.* It's that simple.

Let's look at a young man by the name of John who just graduated from high school at 18 years of age. He picked up a job as a construction worker making $36,000 a year. One of his big goals is to become financially independent by age 40. How does he get there?

John starts working back in time, taking that long-term goal and breaking it down into specific short-term goals that take him to where he wants to go by age 40. The question is, "How does John get to where he wants to go based on where he currently finds himself?"

He decides that $500,000 will get the job done in 22 years as he lives frugally and ends up marrying the right person (or not), manages inflation as best he can, and realizes that he will still work at that time, but it will be something he loves (he is still trying to figure out what that thing is). Next up, how much to save and where?

John gets out a compound interest calculator and starts running some numbers. Of course, he has read *What Color is the Sky*, so he knows how to invest wisely in no-load index mutual funds to keep the cost very low. He also knows that the historical return on the U.S. stock market has been around 10% over the last 90 years.

John decides to use 9% as a reasonable expected AFTER cost return on his stock portfolio that is over weighted to small companies and value companies and diversified all over the world in developed and developing countries. He has set aside $3,000 in a Short-Term Bond Index Fund for emergencies. The rest will be going to his stock mutual funds.

John figures out he can reach $501,214.22 at age 40 if he saves $600 per month into his tax-sheltered accounts. That ends up being 20% of his gross paycheck. If he wants to get there faster, he saves more money and maybe picks up income elsewhere. He is also counting on small raises over time, which should help him increase his savings as he focuses on always saving 20% of his paycheck month after month.

So, did you just read that story about John and find reasons why you couldn't do what he did OR did you see how you could do something similar based on your own situation? Finding solutions will help you reach your goals in life. Identifying roadblocks and seeing yourself as a victim will stop you. Which type of person are you going to be? The choice is yours. The choice is always yours.

"Often we are caught in a mental trap of seeing enormously successful people and thinking they are where they are because they have some special gift. Yet a closer look shows that the greatest gift that extraordinarily successful people have over the average person is their ability to get themselves to take action."

- **Anthony Robbins**

48

SAVING PART II

How does someone become a saver when he or she is surrounded by people who like to spend? Many people must deal with this issue after getting that diploma. It all starts with the right goals and the right mindset (with a bit of stubbornness thrown in).

The real question probably is, "How does a person break away from the pack?" That is easy to say, but hard to do. Sadly, many people might make fun of you for saving your money. They might call you a nerd or some other name that is meant to put you down.

Ignore them. People who save their money are the ones who get ahead in life and the ones who don't, stay where they are. It's kind of like some friend who is getting an F in some class saying, "You are weird for getting a passing grade." The future will not be kind to those who get F's.

Freedom comes to those who save their money. Being a slave to a job is what comes to those who choose not to save. The earlier you get started saving your money, the faster you will get to the wonderful destination called financial freedom. You can do this!

How do you become a great saver? You automate it and pay yourself first. Keep this simple so you can sustain it for a very long time. You make sure that money comes out of your paycheck or your bank account as soon as you get paid. Have it go to your retirement plan at work (401k for example), a Roth IRA or taxable account at Vanguard, and/or an emergency account at a credit union.

How much should you save from each paycheck? 20% of your gross income (before tax is withheld) is the number to shoot for. If you are highly motivated, select 30%. Don't let the percentages scare you off. Identify the numbers and get it done. Let's take a look at an example.

If you make $2,500 per month, you would save $500 per month to equal 20%. That would be $750 per month at 30%. You become a great saver one month at a time. What you have left is what you get to spend. Save first, spend last in that order.

What if you can't save that much each month? Save what you can. If you can only save 5%, then save 5%. Automate it and pay yourself first into those retirement accounts as if you were saving 20%. Every little bit counts. ALWAYS save money out of each paycheck.

Gradually increase that amount over time. Increase your savings by at least 1% every January and try to make it 2%. Increase it by 3% if you can. Push yourself a bit and one day, you will find that you are saving 20% of your gross income.

Here is one final point on becoming a great saver. Surround yourself with other great savers. They will lift you up. You could have a little competition on who will save the most either by dollar amount or percentage of income. In the end, you all will win.

The group of people that you allow into your life will impact your future in some pretty profound ways. Make sure the right people are entering and if necessary, let others leave. Financial freedom awaits those who take control of their money and their life. Make that YOU.

"While successful financial planning requires attention to several important areas, including getting your debt under control and maintaining sufficient insurance coverage, none is more important than saving regularly and investing those savings wisely."

- **Jonathan D. Pond**, *Grow Your Money*

49

SAVING PART III

Some of you will have debt up to your eyeballs and saving money may seem like a far-off dream. I get it, but there is still a path for you to reach financial freedom. It will take a bit longer and it will surely be more difficult, but it can be done by those who are properly motivated and stick with it over time.

Many people leave college with a diploma and mounds of debt as they "do what they were supposed to do." If that is you, it's time to get a plan to pay that off before the small hill of loans becomes the big mountain that looks unclimbable. Dealing with it now will reduce the pain. Ignoring it, will increase the agony.

You can still save 20% or more per month by putting those savings toward your debt. You just put that savings into the debts instead of your retirement accounts and emergency fund. You save by paying off your debt at an accelerated rate. There is one exception and it's important to know that before proceeding forward.

If you are offered matching money at work with your retirement plan, GET IT. *Do not turn down FREE money*. Getting a guaranteed 100% or 50% return on your money is something you should not pass up. Whether your employer matches dollar for dollar or fifty cents on the dollar, make sure you save what is needed to get the free money.

After the matching is accomplished, save about $1,000 and put it in the bank for emergencies. If possible, see if mom and dad could serve as your emergency account while you go on this debt reduction journey. If so, take that $1,000 and put it toward your debts.

Next up, save at least 20% and put it toward your debts. Use the debt snowball or the debt avalanche as you save 20% above and beyond the minimum payments that are due. These extra payments on debt are a form of savings where you can get guaranteed rates of return.

If you are paying extra on a 6.8% student loan, you are earning that rate of return with each extra dollar you put down. There is no better deal on planet earth. Paying extra on those debts and earning high guaranteed rates of return will very quickly improve your financial situation.

Once you get to the low interest rate loans, you might decide to stop paying extra on your debts and start saving into your retirement account at work, a Roth IRA outside of work and/or your savings account for emergencies. Remember to consistently evaluate the opportunity costs with every dollar you have coming into your life.

There is a path toward becoming free of your debt as you save into it over the necessary period of time. It all comes down to you and what you're going to do about it. No one is going to come in and save the day. YOU save the day and you can month after month after month. Financial freedom is waiting for you. Go get it!

"Credit card debt is the exact opposite of a great investment. Wouldn't you like to have an investment that compounded at such a rapid rate? Of course you would. We all would. At 18 percent, a debt doubles in just four years—and then redoubles again in the next four years. Ouch! That's four times as much debt in just eight years--and it's still compounding! That compounding is why banks have distributed credit cards so widely to people they don't even know. And that's why you should never ever use any credit card debt."

- **Burton Malkiel and Charles Ellis**, *The Elements of Investing*

50

INVESTING PART I

Investing your money requires you to risk temporary loss based on market speculation. It is important to understand the difference between saving money and investing it. You save money into accounts for your future needs. Investing requires you to take a certain degree of risk.

Okay, that was some verbiage you might find in a textbook that may or may not make much sense to you. Here's the same thing in basic English. You want to become a smart investor so your savings will grow faster than your living expenses and you're not stuck living paycheck to paycheck in a crummy job that sucks.

Let's start with the basics. Investing is not gambling if you know what you are doing. You simply take short-term risk (your account can go down in value based on the stock and/or bond markets going down in value) for long-term gain (you end up with a pot of money at the end of the rainbow that will be used to pay the bills after you quit working).

Stocks have been the best way to grow your money over time beyond inflation (the cost of goods and services goes up). What is a stock? A business goes public and offers a small share of the company to you and me. We buy that stock giving the business capital to grow and in return, we are reimbursed over time through their dividends and earnings growth.

We reduce the risk of loss (the business goes bankrupt for example) by owning thousands of stocks instead of one. Owning a mutual fund that pools money from many people provides us the opportunity to own stock in many businesses. Ultimately, we end up making money based on how all those businesses do over time.

Some mutual funds own stocks in the United States. Some own stocks outside the United States. Some own bonds issued by governments and corporations, which is debt that promises a specified interest rate. Some mutual funds own stocks and bonds.

Some mutual funds are very broad (owning all publicly traded companies in the United States for example) and some are very specific (owning only stock in health care and technology companies for example). There are thousands of mutual funds!

Which mutual funds should you own? *You want to own the funds that have kicked ass over the last 40 years.* Those funds are called no-load index mutual funds that own entire markets. Those types of funds will own stocks, bonds, and/or a combination of stocks and bonds.

Why are they so good? It primarily comes down to cost. You pay no load (no commission) as you eliminate the middle man and then you pay a very low yearly fee (expense ratio) to the mutual fund manager(s) based on the limited trading within the fund.

Why doesn't everyone own index funds? There are millions of dollars in advertising spent by the financial services industry trying to convince you that they are better at managing your money. The evidence clearly states they are not. Informed investors know that.

Which specific index funds should you own? The short answer is a Total Stock Market Index Fund that owns the entire U.S. economy. Keep reading for more details and more options. The truth is out there for those who are willing to look for it. Go find it!

"Most investors, both institutional and individual, will find the best way to own common stocks is through an index fund that charges minimal fees. Those following this path are sure to beat the net results (after fees and expenses) delivered by the great majority of investment professionals."

- **Warren Buffett**

51

INVESTING PART II

You will have many opportunities to invest your money and there are A LOT of people who are anxious to "help" you. You should avoid most of the options out there and most of the people trying to assist you. In most cases, those **"helpers"** are simply trying to get their hand in your pockets. Swat them away and educate yourself elsewhere. Here is a primer for two different types of people.

The *risk taker* (dominated by young men) likes to "shoot for the moon" as they try to get rich fast. They think they are smarter than others. *Overconfidence* will reduce their returns over time. They tend to trade often and focus on individual stocks in many cases. **Big mistake!** The mindset needs to change if this type of person wants success over time with their investing dollars. Emotions are your enemy.

The *fearful one* (dominated by young women) *lacks confidence* in their abilities and therefore, does nothing. Or worse, runs to the "helpers" who guarantee certain rates of return. They don't know what they are doing and they don't think they can learn about this complicated issue. **Wrong!** YOU can become a great investor with the right education. The key is to find the right teachers. Emotions are your enemy.

Which group do you fall into? Be honest with that person in the mirror. **Knowing thyself will make you a better investor**. It is the starting point when it comes to this investing game. Whether you are the risk taker, the fearful one, or somewhere in-between, you can change. That's right, you can become a great investor by educating yourself on the issue and on what has worked and what has not worked in the past.

Here is what you **should do:** (1) Own stocks, bonds, and real estate that produce yearly income. (2) Go heavy on stocks when you are young because of your long time horizon. (3) Invest your money in mutual funds that own thousands of stocks and/or bonds that make up entire markets. (4) Own investments inside and outside the country where you live. (5) Invest in index mutual funds to reduce cost. (6) Feed those accounts every month with each paycheck. (7) Start as early as possible. (8) Stay the course.

Here is what you **should not do:** (1) Buy individual stocks and bonds. (2) Buy Gold and Silver. (3) Invest in life insurance products. (4) Attend free dinners. (5) Seek out help from fee-based helpers. (6) Listen to the "noise" of the daily markets. (7) Listen to the media. (8) Listen to people who predict the future. (9) Think you are smarter than the next guy. (10) Allow your emotions to creep into your decision-making.

Read those last two paragraphs again and follow the advice closely. Educate yourself in more depth by reading *The Investor's Manifesto* by William Bernstein. Also, go to *Investing 101*, at thecrazymaninthepinkwig.com. Investing your money does not have to be difficult or time consuming. I spend less than 10 minutes A YEAR on my investments. So can you.

You can become the wise and successful investor once you understand the environment, YOU, and what path has been the successful path walked by many in the past. Find that path, get on that path, stay on that path (be aware that others will try to knock you off that path), and finally, circle back and show others that path. Go!

"You don't need 99.9% of what Wall Street is selling. It's expensive, unsuitable, or stupid. Most investments are designed to profit the brokers, banks, and insurance companies, not you. They should carry a warning label, "Beware! This financial product may be injurious to your wealth!"

- **Jane Bryant Quinn**

52

INVESTING PART III

Did you wonder what I meant in that last chapter when I mentioned the "helpers?" These are the people who say they are trying to help you, but they really aren't. They are just helping themselves at your expense using your money to do it. You must learn to say NO to most of the helpers in the financial services industry and that is a pretty big list of people and organizations.

Most of the helpers in the financial services industry are fee-based advisors in one form or another. Fee-based? They make money in many ways that are generally hidden from view. Long ago the industry figured out that people don't like getting a bill so they hatched an idea to "bake" the costs into the products. It worked, FOR THEM. *Just because you don't cut them a check doesn't mean you aren't paying them.* You are.

In most cases, your local life insurance agent and financial advisor work for someone else as they spend time convincing you they work for you. The costs are hidden so you feel like you are not paying them, but believe me, you are paying them. The system has been built for them, not you. P.S. They may be very nice people, but that does not mean they deserve a cut of your investment dollars.

So, what's the point of this chapter? (1) Stop looking at these financial people as experts on finance. They are not experts in the vast majority of cases. If they are experts at anything, it is sales. (2) If you need help with your investments, take your time and educate yourself carefully on where to go and where not to go. There is a limited amount of good resources that will actually help you.

Educate yourself prior to seeking assistance. You might just realize you can do this yourself. Many people can, once they overcome their fears and lack of understanding on the issue of money and how to grow it over time. You can become your own financial advisor. Keep that point in mind as you gain knowledge on this rather mystifying subject.

If you need help, seek the assistance of a *fee-only* advisor and don't pay very much when you do. Fee-only advisor? Someone who gets paid by you and only you. That person works for no one except you. You want someone who is a true fiduciary who does what is in your best interest instead of theirs or some large company.

Where? Most people just starting out who desire help would be wise to consider one of the robo-advisors if they need help with their investment accounts. Robo-advisor? These online advisors invest your money using evidence based algorithms at a low cost. Basically, a robot becomes your advisor and charges you a minimal fee.

If you need help in managing your money, go to Wealthfront.com or Betterment.com. The yearly cost ranges from .25% to .35% and the underlying costs of the funds (the expense ratio) will run you another .12% or so. Total costs should come in at .37% to .47% as of 01 January 2017. That's not bad if you are needing help and willing to pay for it.

Wealthfront seems to be a good place to start for those who are starting with a small amount of money. With as little as $500 you can open an account and they waive their .25% yearly fee for the first $15,000 in the account. All you pay is the .12% for the underlying fees on the low-cost funds. That's hard to beat IF you need help.

"A vast industry of stockbrokers, financial planners, and investment advisers skims a fortune for themselves off the top in exchange for passing their clients' money on to people who, as a whole, cannot possibly outperform the market."
                              - **Michael Lewis**

53

THE TRANSFER

You are probably going to work at many locations in your lifetime. It would be wise to transfer your old retirement accounts to <u>Vanguard.com</u> and into index funds when you leave a job. Vanguard will walk you through the process at no cost. It will require a basic understanding of what you have, where it is, and what type of an account the money is in.

Many people will have pre-tax money in a traditional retirement plan like a 401(k), 403(b), TSP, or 457. You could possibly have a defined benefit plan (pension) that could be moved. Whatever you have, identify whether it is pre-tax or after tax and get the ball rolling. Contact Vanguard either by phone or online and start the transfer process.

Transfer pre-tax retirement money to a Traditional IRA to avoid any tax consequences. Move after tax retirement money to a Roth IRA in the same way. Make this as simple and painless as you can. Move the money from one institution to another electronically, without it ever touching your hands. Easy peasy.

What investments should you select when making these moves? Now, *that is an important question.* You will want to step back and think about whether you need more stocks or bonds in your portfolio prior to making that decision. There is no perfect answer that fits everyone in all situations, but here are a few pointers on asset allocation.

Keep your stock allocation at least at 50%, and consider raising it to 80% or more when you are young. Diversify all over the world. Avoid a portfolio that has all bonds. Inflation will eat it up faster than a five-year-old with an ice cream cone. **Owning stocks reduces inflation risk.**

ALWAYS focus on cost when transferring money. Here are three Vanguard no-load index funds that will serve you well for years to come: **Total Stock Market Index Fund, Total International Stock Index Fund** and **Total Bond Market Index Fund**. If you move more than $10,000 into one of those funds, you will get the low cost Admiral Shares.

If you prefer, buy one or two target retirement funds that own multiple index funds. A Target Retirement 2040 Fund will own a great deal more stocks than a Target Retirement 2020 Fund. Take a little time to identify how each fund is allocated between stocks and bonds so you can make an informed decision on which fund is right for you.

This information applies to your current employer when you leave, but it also applies to past employers. Corral that money that is floating around out there from previous jobs and move it to Vanguard index funds for consolidation, simplicity, low cost and much higher returns over time. YOU must take control of the situation.

DO NOT cash out your retirement accounts when you leave a job. You will incur a big tax bill if the money is in pre-tax accounts and you will pay a big fat penalty to the government for taking the money out before age 59.5. You want to keep that money sheltered from taxes as long as possible, which is why you transfer the money and never touch it. Make it happen!

"So to realize the winning returns generated by businesses over the long term, the intelligent investor will minimize to the bare bones the costs of financial intermediation. That's what common sense tells us. That's what indexing is all about."

- **John Bogle,** *The Little Book of Common Sense Investing*

54

INSURANCE PART I

This topic is one that most people shy away from. Why? It is a necessary evil and much of the time it deals with loss, death, pain and suffering. Yikes! Let's try to take the emotions out of this discussion and simply deal with the facts and what you need to know so you can make an informed decision on your insurance needs based on your own situation.

Buy insurance to deal with catastrophes only. DO NOT buy insurance to deal with the small things in life. This approach will eliminate most insurance policies and allow you to focus only on the ones you need. When buying insurance, get those deductibles as high as possible ($1,000 will do) and file a claim only when something big happens.

Why should the deductibles be so high? The higher the deductible, the lower your yearly premiums you will pay for the coverage. You will pay less and still be covered if you have some type of catastrophic event. Cover the small stuff out of your emergency account. That is also the place you retrieve the $1,000 when needed to pay a deductible.

When needing insurance, be wary of your local insurance agent. Many of them will try to sell you CRAP you don't need. Why? They make big fat commissions on insurance policies that have a high likelihood of not paying out. Once you know what you need, seek quotes from independent agents that offer you estimations from many companies.

The whole world of insurance can be quite mystifying. Learn more on this subject of insurance by reading *Personal Finance for Dummies* by Eric Tyson and *Making the Most of Your Money* by Jane Bryant Quinn. Those two independent sources will educate you without selling you.

You need health, automobile, and home (that is if you own a car and a home). Any incident involving your health or your property can devastate you financially. Always make sure you have the proper amount of insurance in those areas as you head out into the world.

You need health insurance so a hospital stay doesn't devastate you. You need automobile insurance so an accident doesn't ruin you (*consider* liability only when the value of your vehicle goes below $5,000). You need home insurance so mother nature doesn't kick you to the curb.

You *might* need life insurance. Life insurance should be purchased to provide for the people who count on you financially, such as a spouse or children. It doesn't include a goldfish or a dog. More on life insurance in the next chapter.

What about disability insurance? Some smart and informed people say you need it. I'm not so sure. I basically don't trust insurance companies to pay out without fighting you tooth and nail over it. It can be quite expensive based on the kind of work you do. Weigh all your options before deciding on a disability policy.

The insurance companies have the numbers on their side, which is to say, they are the casino and their clients are the gamblers. Consider taking the premiums you would have paid on policies you don't need and instead, pay down debt and/or invest for your future needs in those low-cost index funds. Make yourself the casino!

"Life insurance is, though unnecessarily, one of the most expensive parts of a good financial plan. To wrestle control of your insurance policy and premiums away from your insurance company and agent, you must understand how the system works."

- **Charles Givens**, *Financial Self-Defense*

55

INSURANCE PART II

You need to buy life insurance if someone would suffer financially if you died. That is the responsible thing to do. If no one relies on you financially, it is unlikely you need life insurance. Single people with no kids don't need life insurance in most cases.

Avoid discussing this issue with your local life insurance agent. The system is built for the life insurance industry, not you. The insurance company puts that agent in an uncomfortable position as they send them out into the field looking for victims; I mean clients. Avoid buying financial products from commissioned based life insurance agents.

Hit on the *life insurance basics* link at thecrazymaninthepinkwig.com to learn more. A life insurance agent has a conflict of interest with what is sold. They earn big commissions by selling high cost whole life, variable life, and universal life, while earning small commissions selling term life. What do you think they are going to recommend?

If you do need life insurance, go to Term4sale.com and buy an inexpensive term policy AFTER you have reviewed how much Social Security would pay out and AFTER you have reviewed any free life insurance benefit provided by your employer. It is important to identify what you have first before forking out money for more.

Social Security? Social Security provides survivor benefits to a spouse and children if one spouse dies. Survivor benefits kick in when you have children in the home. Go to socialsecurity.gov and print off your statement to review your *survivor benefits*. You could have over $500,000 in survivor benefits. That is a FREE life insurance policy!

Should you get life insurance on a child? Hell, no! Children cost you money, they don't make you money. If you want to save some money for their future needs, do it in a 529 College Plan (go straight to the state, while avoiding an advisor) or some taxable account at Vanguard that will grow the money at a much faster rate than any crappy life insurance policy.

How much life insurance should you get if you need it? It will vary and it certainly is not a precise science. Again, I would avoid asking this question to a life insurance agent. The more you buy, the more they earn. The conflict of interest continues to pop up again and again when sitting down with a commission based salesperson.

A basic rule of thumb would have you replacing your income by six times. If you earn $50,000 a year, you would consider having $300,000 in coverage for example. Of course, identify how much you have at Social Security and work before buying extra amounts. You might have all you need at those two locations without looking elsewhere.

Is life insurance taxed when a loved one receives the death benefit? In almost all cases life insurance payouts *are not taxable*. Educate your family on what to do with the funds if that day ever comes. Have that discussion now when emotions are not so high and people can think straight. It's time to take control!

"You are engaged in a life-and-death struggle with the financial services industry. Every dollar in fees, expenses, and spreads you pay them comes directly out of your pocket. If you act on the assumption that every broker, insurance salesman, mutual fund salesperson, and financial advisor you encounter is a hardened criminal, you will do just fine."

- **William Bernstein**, *The Investor's Manifesto*

56

INSURANCE PART III

This last chapter on insurance deals specifically with an insurance product. It's called an annuity. Life insurance agents and brokers love to sell annuities. Why? Once again, it comes down to those big fat commissions. Products are created by the insurance industry to make money off of you, not for you. Never forget that.

Many smart people throughout America buy those crappy annuities. Why? I would say there are two primary reasons. (1) Many policies provide a guaranteed return and people like guaranteed returns even if they are small and there is a lot of fine print. (2) Life insurance agents are very good at selling and they can make just about anything sound good. Especially when it pays THEM a lot of money.

Stay away from the free dinners that many life insurance agents provide. Free dinners? You might get something in the mail that invites you to a free dinner by some life insurance agent/financial advisor as they provide "financial education" on some type of product or service. That financial education will cost you dearly. It is nothing more than a sales pitch and the product is usually an annuity. Run away!

Be mindful of the latest and greatest sales pitch. You might hear some agent say that annuities are generally bad, but he or she is selling a "good" one. That's garbage, even if the agent believes their own pitch. Some salesperson might show you a print out on how much your money could grow over many years. What the agent projects and what you get can be two very different things. Ignore those numbers.

Here is the bottom line on annuities and the salespeople who peddle them. Life insurance companies love them because they make them a lot of money as they use your funds to make them rich. Life insurance agents love them because they pay big commissions and then they get awards and bonuses if they sell more of that CRAP than others do.

What do YOU get? A product where your investment is locked up for many years (7 to 10 is normal). If you pull your money out in those early years, you will pay a big penalty. If you keep your money in there for a long period of time, you will end up with piss poor returns that might stay up with inflation if you're lucky. Neither option is good for you.

If you want decent returns on your money, invest in no-load stock and bond index mutual funds. Eliminate the middleman, which in turn reduces the cost to you in a dramatic way. Diversification and lower cost will help you build your wealth over time. It's pretty darn simple. *Compound money in your account, not someone else's.*

They win and you lose. That is how the game is played if you end up spending time with a life insurance agent. So, don't. Never invest in life insurance products (the immediate annuity *could* be an exception, but that applies to old people, not young people). Your returns are dramatically reduced because of the costs. Don't play their game. Play your game!

"Beware of brokers and insurance agents eager to escort your cash to another annuity. Investors get switched from one mediocre annuity to another all the time because brokers receive healthy commissions every time they convince someone to jump."

- **Daniel Solin**, *The Smartest Retirement Book You'll Ever Read*

57

BUYING A VEHICLE PART I

Should you buy a vehicle soon after landing that first decent paying job. Do you need one? Notice I am not asking if you want one. We all, most likely, want a vehicle that is newer than the one we have. Hence, the distinction between a want and a need.

You need a vehicle when you don't have one and one is required to get you somewhere like a job. You need a vehicle when the one you have is falling apart and costing you a small fortune in repair bills. So, what type of vehicle do you need? That's where it gets more difficult to figure out.

No human being needs a brand new vehicle. Again, they may want one, but they don't need one. So, when you go about deciding on the vehicle you need, focus on the important things and pay less attention to the unimportant. Important? How much will it cost upfront and how much will the ongoing yearly costs run you?

Car companies learned long ago that it's easier selling a car using the monthly payment as the main criteria instead of the actual price of the car. Psychologically, it is easier on the buyer to pay $380 a month rather than $25,000 on a 5-year loan at 5.9%. If you looked carefully at the actual numbers, it might just cause you to spend less money. Hmm…

What is best for the car company is not what is best for you. Don't let them brainwash you into thinking like they want you to think. That means putting less focus on that monthly payment and more emphasis on the total cost of the vehicle and if a loan is taken out, how long and at what interest rate. This is how YOU take control of the situation.

Here is a good rule of thumb. Only buy a vehicle when you need one. Don't buy a vehicle simply because you want one to replace a vehicle that you have gotten tired of owning. Newer vehicles are expensive upfront and expensive to own based on the yearly registration and insurance costs. And let's not forget the depreciation.

Depreciation? New cars depreciate a great deal in value, especially in the first two years of ownership. A $30,000 new car could be worth less than $20,000 after two years. You just lost over $10,000! Cars are expensive and the newer they are, the more they will cost you in upfront money and over time as well, based on insurance and registration costs.

Vehicles are wealth depleting assets that affect your financial situation in a negative way. You want to buy vehicles as infrequently as possible. The more vehicle purchases you have in your lifetime, the more money you are going to lose. Don't let others convince you that buying cars often is a good idea. It isn't. So, what is a person to do?

Buy a decent vehicle, take care of it, and then drive it for long periods of time (at least 10 years). The longer you drive that vehicle, the less it will hurt your bottom line. Get this issue straight in your mind prior to reading the next two chapters. **Vehicles suck money from me.** Your job is to reduce the damage as best you can.

"You don't need a fancy car to impress people for business purposes. Some people I know say that they absolutely must drive a nice, brand spanking new car to set the right impression for business purposes… consider that if clients and others see you driving an expensive new car they may think that you spend money wastefully or that you're getting rich off of them!"

- **Eric Tyson,** *Personal Finance for Dummies*

58

BUYING A VEHICLE PART II

So, let's say you need a car, where should a person start? The internet is the answer. Most of the time spent on buying a vehicle should be in the preparation phase. Research as much as possible about the type of vehicle you are looking to buy. Be patient with this process as you gather the knowledge to make an informed decision.

There are important questions to answer prior to entering a car lot. The car lot should be the end of the process. You only go there to test drive a vehicle that you have researched thoroughly. You then negotiate the price based on what you know it is worth based on your research. A quick trip to a mechanic you trust would be wise as well.

Before we get to the questions, let's cover other information. You can buy from a private party or a car dealer. *You will likely get a better deal from a private party who is not a professional.* You are not going to get some great deal at a dealership. You are going to get screwed at the dealership. Just try to get screwed as little as possible.

You can buy used or new or lease. Leasing is usually the worst financial decision. New is next and used is usually the best if you know what you are doing and are careful as you go through the process. Depreciation is the main reason why the used vehicle is the better deal. Also, the ongoing costs will be lower with a quality used vehicle.

If you end up buying a used vehicle from a private party or dealer, have that vehicle checked out carefully by a mechanic that you trust. If the other party won't let you do that, walk away. You want to know everything you possibly can about any future issues that vehicle may have.

Spend weeks and/or months researching everything you need to know about the vehicle that you want to buy. Where do you go to do that research? Kellybluebook.com and Edmunds.com are two good sites. Also, my website will work. Hit on the menu and then the *buying a car* link to increase your knowledge. YouTube.com might help as well.

Keep researching cars that interest you as you work at answering the questions you see below. Gathering this information will give you the confidence you will need to help you through this grueling process. Next up, do you need a loan?

When possible, pay cash for a vehicle. Paying cash will cause you to spend less in almost all cases. If you do need a loan, get pre-qualified at a local Credit Union. They will generally offer you the best interest rate on a vehicle loan whether you choose new or used.

What is the best financial way to buy a vehicle? Buy a quality 3 or 4-year-old vehicle from a private party (less markup for profit) and then have the vehicle checked out carefully by a trusted mechanic. Allow someone else to lose big time on depreciation. Now, the questions.

- How much cash do you have available for a car purchase?
- How much are you willing to pay for a vehicle?
- Are you going to buy used or new?
- What kind of vehicle would you prefer?
- Why are you choosing that kind of vehicle?
- What is the value of the specific vehicle you are researching?
- What will that vehicle cost you in yearly registration fees?
- What will that vehicle cost you in yearly insurance?
- What is the safety record on that type of vehicle?
- How much is routine maintenance for this kind of vehicle?

"Education is the key to unlock the golden door of freedom."

- **George Washington Carver**

59

BUYING A VEHICLE PART III

You have done your research. You know the vehicle that you want and have found it on a car lot via the internet. Your research tells you that the 4-year old vehicle that you like is worth $17,500. The dealer is selling it for $18,900. That is a difference of $1,400. You decide you are willing to pay $18,000 in cash for this vehicle (don't tell the dealer this information).

Prior to making an appointment with the dealer, you have also identified the value of your vehicle, which is gradually falling apart, which is why you are seeking a better vehicle. Your research tells you your vehicle is worth $3,800 and will be a possible bargaining tool in the negotiation. So will the $15,000 you have saved up in the bank for this purchase.

You have been to the Credit Union with a credit score of 770 and they tell you they will give you a 3.99% loan on a used vehicle that is 4 years old. Since you are earning .5% on your savings, you have decided to use the cash to buy the car instead of taking out a loan. Because you have planned ahead, you have many good options to consider prior to the negotiation.

You have contacted your insurance agent and you know how much that newer vehicle will cost you to insure. You have identified how much the registration fee will be in the first year and following years. The vehicle has very low mileage for a 4-year-old car and the safety record for that type of vehicle is excellent. It's time to call the dealer and make an appointment.

You meet with the dealer and take the car for a spin. Everything looks and feels great. He asks you what you want your monthly payment to be. You tell him that is not how you negotiate. You will be negotiating on the price of the entire car. Monthly payments are meaningless to you.

You tell the dealer you would like to borrow the car for about two hours so your mechanic can go over it carefully. The dealer says their mechanic already has and it is in perfect shape. You say thanks, but you have your own mechanic and you want to hear it from him, not the guy who works at the dealership (and gets paid by the dealership).

Two hours later you come back to the dealer and identify two small parts that need to be replaced soon. The cost with labor will be $240 (you got that information from your mechanic). You tell the salesman you are willing to make him an offer today. First, he says they have looked at your car and say they will give you $4,000 for it ($200 above fair value).

You tell him thanks, but first, you want to focus on the asking price of the dealer's vehicle. He says they might drop the price to $18,500. You say $17,500 is fair and you are willing to pay that right now. He steps out to talk to his manager. He comes back and says the manager won't budge. You leave the salesman your contact information and head home.

Your ability to leave puts you in charge of the situation instead of him. Detaching yourself emotionally from the result puts you in the drivers seat. There will be other vehicles. Three days later the salesman calls you and says they can go down to $18,000. You tell him he has a deal at $14,000 with the $4,000 they will give you on your trade-in. He says okay.

Did you get some amazing deal at the expense of the dealer? No. The dealer made some money and you didn't get screwed too bad. You end up paying the dealer $14,000 in cash, keeping $1,000 in the bank for emergencies, which you will build back up over time. In the meantime, you got yourself a better car that you will drive for over 10 years. Well done!

"Knowledge is power. Information is liberating. Education is the premise of progress, in every society, in every family."

- **Kofi Annan**

60

BUYING A HOME PART I

Should you buy a home soon after landing that first job that pays you the big bucks? Probably not, is the short answer. The longer answer will follow. What is important on this issue, is properly educating yourself from the right sources and steering clear of the wrong sources. P.S. There are a lot more wrong sources.

The right sources? People who are well versed on the subject AND are not selling anything. Here are three good resources: Jane Bryant Quinn, Eric Tyson, and Jonathan Clements. Anything they write is worth reading. The wrong sources? Salespeople, pundits on television, real estate agents, and even family and friends who might be well-meaning, but lack a true understanding on the matter.

Here are the basics when it comes to housing costs that every person should know when receiving a diploma and entering the world. Renting is just fine and it is not throwing money down a gutter (wave people off who say such ridiculous things). For many people in many different situations, renting is exactly the right move to make. DO NOT let others bully you into buying a home until you are ready. Ready?

You are ready to buy a home when you have 20% to put down on the home you want. You are ready when you can see yourself settling down for at least 10 years in that home. You are ready when you have a solid relationship and job. You are ready when you understand that owning a home is expensive and you are going to lose money on it over time. That's right, *a home is not a good investment.*

A home is a bad investment once you consider the yearly costs. The yearly costs? Every year you will pay property taxes and insurance. You will pay to maintain the property (things break and upkeep is needed). You will pay for upgrades (better bathroom, better kitchen, better patio, better floor, etc.). You will pay interest on the loan. Finally, you will need to average out the costs from when you bought and sold the home.

A $200,000 home could easily cost you 10% a year. That equals $20,000 PER YEAR in costs. Even if you made 4% per year in appreciation (far from guaranteed) with a bit of a tax deduction, you will still lose money once those yearly costs are factored in. Here is the bottom line that we all should have been told at a young age: **Homeownership is expensive.** Buy a home to raise a family, not as an investment. It is a bad investment.

You are *not ready* if you don't have 20% saved up. You are *not ready* if you haven't learned how to save money consistently every month. You are *not ready* if you expect to move in the next few years. You are *not ready* if you want to stay flexible on where you work and where you live. You are *not ready* when your relationship is a bit rocky. Homeownership is stressful. Go into it knowing that.

Do you have to buy a home? Hell, no! Can you rent your entire life and do just fine financially? Hell, yes! Remind yourself about that key point when you hear others telling you why you should buy a home. In many cases, they are simply repeating a mantra that they have heard in their lifetime, without running the numbers. Buying a home is an option, not a requirement. If you want to rent, go ahead and rent.

"A home is not a good financial investment and never was. But a home can certainly be a fine investment in your families happiness…"

- **Charles Ellis,** *Winning the Loser's Game*

61

BUYING A HOME PART II

If you do want to buy a home, where do you start? *You start by becoming a good saver.* This means you have learned to live far below your means. Far below your means? You can live on 50% of your gross income, which of course you understand after reading the chapter on the 50/50 rule. If you make $60,000 a year, you live on $30,000.

Are you there yet? If not, continue to work on that habit while you rent an apartment, condo or house. I would not buy a home until you can get to that point. What happens if you don't? You don't buy a home. It's that simple. You're just not ready to own a home based on your habits that make up your life. Be patient with this process.

So, let's say you are there. You are living on 50% of your gross income, what next? Do you have 20% to put down on the down payment? If not, you're not ready. You have not saved up enough to avoid Private Mortgage Insurance (PMI), which will increase the cost of the home with higher payments each month until you hit 20% equity in the home.

Now, you could decrease the size of the home, thereby reducing the cost, thereby having 20% to put down on the place. That's just fine. That means you *could* be ready *if* you have the money needed to avoid PMI. You either have 20% to put down on the home or you don't. You are either ready to be a homeowner or you're not.

Let's look at some real numbers. Let's say you want to buy a $200,000 home. You will need $40,000 for the down payment (20% of $200,000). You look at your savings and you're at $20,000. You cannot afford the $200,000 home.

You can afford a $100,000 home with your savings. What happens if you don't want the $100,000 home? Keep saving until you hit $40,000 and can afford the $200,000 home. Don't complicate this issue and don't let others rush you into something you are not ready to do. Become a consistent saver and be patient.

Now, let's say you have reached $40,000 in your savings and you are ready to buy the home you really want. What next? Go to your local lenders to see what kind of loans they are offering at the time. Keep in mind, there are many variables based on when you are considering buying the home. Saying that, here are a few basics.

Get your credit scores (husband and wife) to 760 to get the lowest interest rates. Get quotes from multiple lenders in your area on a 15 or 30-year fixed rate loan. The 15-year loan will save you many thousands of dollars over time and the interest rate should be lower. If you cannot squeeze into the 15-year loan, the 30-year loan will do.

Tell the lenders what you can afford. Don't let them tell you. Put yourself in the driver's seat instead of them. They may be willing to lend you $300,000. So what. You decide the amount, not them. Also, do not let them sell you on a 2nd mortgage to cover the down payment. That's for people who are not ready to buy a home. You are prepared!

"Don't trust a lender when he tells you what you can afford according to some formulas the bank uses to figure out what kind of a credit risk you are. To determine how much a potential home buyer can borrow, lenders look primarily at annual income; they pay no attention to some major aspects of a borrower's overall financial situation… Only you can figure out how much you can afford, because only you know what your other financial goals are and how important they are to you."

- **Eric Tyson,** *Personal Finance for Dummies*

62

BUYING A HOME PART III

Let's say you have the down payment that you need on the home you can afford. What next? You find a lender with the best interest rate as you walk in with credit scores over 760. Next up? Identify the home you want to live in for at least 10 years (if you cannot see yourself living there that long, I would keep renting).

Do you get a Real estate agent to help you find a home or do you look around yourself? That is up to you. A good agent can help you find homes that fit your price range, but keep in mind, the agent works off commissions so they would like to get you in the biggest home possible based on what you can afford. Bigger homes = bigger commissions.

DO NOT let a Real estate agent "squeeze" you into a home beyond what you can afford based on what you have saved up for the down payment. If the most you are willing to pay is $200,000 for example, make that very clear to the agent. You want to see homes at that price range or less. This requires a clear understanding of what you want.

You DO NOT want to see homes beyond that amount. One ploy some agents use to get you in a bigger home (earning them bigger commissions) deals with showing you more expensive homes, hoping you will fall in love with the place. If an agent does that, get another agent.

There are other things to be on the lookout for. Don't fall for the "it won't last long" pitch. They are trying to get you to buy as soon as possible to close the deal. Don't let an agent or lender talk you into that 80/20 mortgage option where you end up putting nothing down, but end up with two loans. No money to put down means you are not ready.

Let's say you have found the home you want. It's time to make an offer. In most cases, it is probably wise to see the Real estate agent as working for the seller. Keep the maximum amount you will pay to yourself. Don't tell the real estate agent. Negotiate with great care to get the best price. That is exactly what the seller will be doing.

Once you end up with a negotiated price, a bunch of other stuff needs to happen. The house needs to be inspected and assessed. The title will need to be authenticated. You will need to set up a closing date. There will be closing costs (which will usually be rolled into the loan). Finally, be sure to make one final walk through just before signing on the dotted line to make sure the home is in the shape you are expecting.

It is a nerve wracking process. You will end up signing many documents at the closing. Most of it will make sense to a lawyer and government regulators. As for you and me, not so much. Don't let them sell you mortgage life insurance at that time. You don't want that expensive policy that pays off your mortgage if you die. If you need life insurance, go get an inexpensive one at term4sale.com. *Avoid mortgage life.*

After all of that, you will move in and think it's done. It isn't. There will be many more costs that you did not see coming. Therefore it is wise to have some cash in the bank after closing. If you don't, you could very well end up putting those unexpected expenses on a credit card. Avoid that by making sure all your cash does not go to the down payment. Buying a home can be a wonderful experience or a nightmare. Make it a good one.

"Don't borrow to the hilt just because a banker says you can. Borrow no more than you feel comfortable repaying. If you buy less house than you can technically afford, you'll have money left over for other investments or for something this book sometimes forgets to mention – fun."

- **Jane Bryant Quinn,** *Making the Most of Your Money*

63

TAXES PART I

Many people know little to nothing about taxes except that they pay too damn much! Rather than complain about taxes, I encourage you to educate yourself on the topic to reduce the tax burden on your life today and your life in the coming decades. Let's start with a few basics. The tax code can and will change over time. The information you see below is current as of January 1, 2017.

You will pay a 7.65% FICA tax (earmarked for Social Security and Medicare) on every dollar you earn from your job. You will pay twice that when you own your own business, but then get a tax credit to get half of it back. You will pay a certain amount of federal income tax based on your income at work. The same goes for state income tax if you work in a state that has one. You might even pay a city income tax if you live in one of the major cities that have one.

You will pay a sales tax (varies by state and city) when you buy items at a store and meals at a restaurant. You will pay a federal and state gas tax when you fill up at the station. You will pay property taxes when you own a home. You will pay registration taxes on your vehicles and other property, which will vary by state. You will pay "sin" taxes when you consume alcohol, cigarettes and other drugs. You will also pay taxes on many other items in life when travelling and simply living.

That's a lot of taxes! Why do I mention them all? *You should know how your life is taxed at every turn if you hope to reduce that burden going forward.* Why would you want to reduce your tax burden? You can take those savings and put them to better use elsewhere in your financial life like paying down debt and increasing savings and/or investments.

Here is some advice. Don't fall into the trap of complaining about taxes. It will do you no good. Now, if you want to support politicians who push for lower taxes, that is certainly your right, but I wouldn't hold your breath. Politicians have a way of saying one thing and doing another.

Here is what you can do. Educate yourself on the subject and then change some of your daily habits in a way that will reduce your yearly tax bill. Reducing your taxes WILL be done by those who are ready to do something about the situation (more to follow in the next chapter).

For instance, you should work at receiving more passive income like long-term capital gains and qualified dividends. Passive income is FICA tax free and taxed at a lower rate in most cases. Here are a few more simple approaches that many people can implement into their life.

- **Invest in your pre-tax retirement plan at work.**
- **Consider other pre-tax accounts at work when offered.**
- **Earn more passive income from your investments.**
- **Own smaller homes.**
- **Buy less expensive cars and do it infrequently.**
- **Buy less stuff.**
- **Eat in restaurants less often.**
- **Drive less often.**
- **Consume drugs less often.**
- **Move to low tax environments.**
- **Avoid high tax environments.**
- **Avoid people who stop you from making these changes.**

"The surest way to grow rich over time is to start by spending a lot less than you make. If you can alter your perspective to be satisfied with what you have, then you won't be as tempted to blow your earnings."

- **Andrew Hallam**, *Millionaire Teacher*

64

TAXES PART II

Your employer will give you a W-4 to fill out when you get hired. *You need to understand your situation prior to filling it out.* The number you put on that form will dictate just how much tax is withheld from your paycheck. And, when applicable, affects your federal, state and city income tax withholding. Here are the basics.

You can put any number you want down or even tax exempt based on your unique status at that time and what you project going forward with your taxes and what will be owed. What should you consider when selecting a number? First, the form provides you a worksheet that could help. You can also go to irs.gov and search for *IRS withholding calculator* to run the numbers electronically.

The withholding number relates to you, how many dependents you have, how many tax deductions you have, and how many tax credits you have. In other words, you could be a single person with a mortgage who puts money into a Traditional 401(k) at work and end up with three allowances on your W-4. You want to take your time to see how many allowances are needed to stop you from getting a big tax refund.

You also do not want to pay a penalty for not having enough taxes withheld. Avoid a penalty by not owing more than $1,000 to the federal government OR you withheld 90% of the tax owed OR you withheld 100% of last year's tax bill. Each state with an income tax may have similar rules, but not necessarily the same. Speak to an accountant to avoid paying penalties to the state and federal governments.

Here are the basics on getting a tax refund. You SHOULD NOT get a big fat tax refund by putting a 0 on your W-4. Why? You have withheld too much in tax all year and then when you file your taxes, the federal and/or state governments simply give you back your money with no interest. That's just dumb.

Increase your allowances as needed so you can do something positive with that money like pay down debt and/or save and invest in retirement accounts. In most cases, you can submit a new W-4, to increase your allowances, whenever you like based on your situation changing. This could happen when you get married, have a child, buy a home, etc...

The opposite would be true if you got divorced, the child is on their own, you quit on the retirement plan, etc. What is important here is the idea that you modify that W-4 as your life changes. DO NOT ask the nice lady in human resources. DO NOT listen to some guy in the breakroom. DO NOT just do what some family member or friend says you should do.

In those cases, it is unlikely any of those people know what your situation is. Just because they have a strong opinion doesn't mean they know what they are talking about. It is crucial that you take the time to understand this issue so you can make the right decision at every point in your future life. Educate yourself and then ACT.

"Infuse your life with action. Don't wait for it to happen. Make it happen. Make your own future. Make your own hope. Make your own love. And whatever your beliefs, honor your creator, not by passively waiting for grace to come down from upon high, but by doing what you can to make grace happen… yourself, right now, right down here on Earth."

- **Bradley Whitford**

65

TAXES PART III

You can and should do your own tax return early in life. It is not as hard and scary as you might think and you will learn a lot. As a matter of fact, it has never been easier thanks to the internet and the software that has been created over time.

Many people can do their own tax return at the federal level and possibly at the state level for FREE. That's right. If your income was below $64,000 in 2016, you will most likely qualify (that number can and usually will change with each passing year). Why pay someone to do something you can do yourself? The answer is, you shouldn't!

You can go to irs.gov and then *freefile* to see the details on how to do it. You can choose from many different companies when deciding which tax program to use. The different programs will walk you through the process step by step and assist you in filing the documents with the IRS. Identify the one you like best and then jump in and get it done.

Why should you take the time to do it yourself? You will learn plenty about your situation and the tax code by doing your own taxes rather than taking your stuff to some person and handing them over with the hope of getting a big refund. The tax preparer is not doing anything special for your very simple tax return.

In many cases, the tax preparer is doing nothing more than taking your information and plugging in the numbers, which again, is something you can do. Filling out tax forms online is not hard, especially when you are young and your situation is simple. It's time to take control of your tax situation and that means doing your own taxes.

So, what do you do if you get a big tax refund? First, don't jump up and down thinking you got over on the government. The government (federal or state) gets over on you when you get a big chunk of money back without interest paid on it. You did something wrong if you get most of your tax withholding back.

If your situation will be similar for next year (meaning that your exemptions, deductions and credits will be about the same), then it's time to increase the number of allowances on your W-4 so you get that refund during the year in monthly increments, rather than the end of the year. *Your paycheck will get bigger as you have less tax withheld.*

If the opposite is true and you owe on your federal tax return (owing under $1,000 on your federal return is a pretty smart strategy as you borrow money from the federal government without paying any interest on the "loan"), reduce the number of allowances on your W-4 as needed. The paycheck will shrink a bit if that happens and that is perfectly okay.

Here is the bottom line when it comes to taxes. They are one of the biggest expenses you will have in your life, probably the biggest. It is important to take an active role in understanding them and then reducing them as best you can. Filing your income tax returns yourself will put you in position to pay less tax. You win in that scenario.

"To do anything truly worth doing, I must not stand back shivering and thinking of the cold and danger, but jump in with gusto and scramble through as well as I can."

- **Og Mandino**

THE

BIG

PICTURE

66

CONSIOUSNESS

To be fully conscious is to be totally alive. This chapter might sound like I am attempting to channel the Buddha, but I can assure you, there is plenty of science behind what I am about to share with you. P.S. This issue has nothing to do with religion, so try to read the next couple of pages with that in mind.

What does it mean to be fully conscious? To be present in the here and now is a simple way to think about it. Don't regret or look longingly into your past. Don't spend your days dreaming about your future. Stay fully present in this moment in time. NOW is all you have. Enjoy it and embrace this beautiful experience. It will soon pass.

Why is this so important? Far too many of us spend too much time thinking about the past and dreaming about the future without fully embracing the present. True happiness can be found in the moment, which is why you and I must find ways to stay in the present without letting our minds leave for some past event or future possibility.

How? The verdict is in and real results have come from meditation. What is meditation? Maybe we should start with what it is not. Meditation is not a religious practice. You can be of any religion or no religion at all to meditate. You don't need to be a monk and dress in a robe or chant while you do it. Meditation can be done by "normal" people.

You simply sit, staying as upright as you can with your posture, and then start breathing in and out, focusing solely on your breath. When your mind wonders, and it will, go back and focus on your breathing. Start with a couple of minutes a day and work up from there.

Why do it? Meditation has been proven through scientific studies to lower your blood pressure, improve your immune system, lessen fear, reduce anxiety and depression, AND increase your energy level and personal well-being. Here is the big message: *Spending a few minutes a day meditating can make your life better.*

Meditation can actually change your brain. That's right. A few minutes each day can literally alter your brain for the better. Why wouldn't someone try that? Probably because they either don't understand the issue and/or they let others tell them how weird it is and how strange YOU are for considering it. Be strange my friend.

So, let's say you are all for improving your brain and lessening the difficulties of life through a bit of meditation. How do you get started? Baby steps is the answer. Let's take me. I started with about five minutes of meditation every day, early in the morning when I woke up. At first, it was kind of hard as I was trying to corral my mind. It gets easier with practice.

After a while, I increased my meditation time to about ten minutes (don't get too caught up with the amount of time; it isn't that important). Over time, I started to look forward to this quiet period as I zoned out all the noise in life and focused on nothing more than my breathing. It calmed me down and I became more mindful by being more present.

You have the power to change what is going on inside of you. Focus your efforts by feeding the mind and the heart with positive thoughts, while discarding the negative ones that continue to pop in to sabotage your thinking. Learn more about this issue with Dan Harris's insightful book, *10% Happier*, or his free app by the same name.

"To enjoy good health, to bring true happiness to one's family, to bring peace to all, one must first discipline and control one's own mind. If a man can control his mind he can find the way to Enlightenment, and all wisdom and virtue will naturally come to him."

- **The Buddha**

67

ENOUGH?

Strive to reach enough in your life and you will end up owning more than just a bunch of stuff. You will own YOU. Enough? The moment in your life where you have enough money and enough possessions so you can stop chasing after those unimportant things and start pursuing something more significant.

This issue can be difficult to fully appreciate when you are a young person. Most young people are grappling with life and just trying to get ahead. Stopping when they have enough is not on their radar. I get that and so, I would like you to consider your future. That is the place where you will have the opportunity to stop because you have enough.

There will come a time for many of you when you reach a level of financial success that affords you the opportunity to stop chasing more. Giving yourself permission to stop pursuing more money and more possessions will free you up to do more to help others. That's right. You spend your days giving instead of chasing after more.

Why? You will do more to help yourself and others as you stop trying to get more stuff and money and instead, find ways to help more people and communities. This kind of thinking requires a real change in how you live your life. Anyone could do it, but the majority do not. Why? Too many people never think they have enough.

So how much is enough? Some people would throw out a dollar amount like $1,000,000. Others would say that is not enough. They would need $10,000,000. Believe it or not, others would say that is not enough. Others would answer the question with a list of possessions.

Some people would need a brand new expensive vehicle. Other people would need a very big and well decorated house. Others would need a full closet full of designer outfits. The list can go on and on if you are not careful. What is needed doesn't have to be what the advertisers tell you it should be. Advertising is all about getting you to reach for more.

Of course, no one needs those items. They just think they do and then soon after they get them, they need other items because what they have now just isn't good enough. That vicious cycle, once again, describes the hedonic treadmill. What was once amazing, is now just ordinary. And off we go to find the next amazing thing.

You are going to see this scenario play out many times in your life as you observe some of the people in your environment chase after more and more and more. Their needs are limitless and yet their happiness is fleeting and always just beyond their grasp. They continue to reach for more instead of being grateful for what they currently have.

You can live a different life. You can work hard. Make a decent living. Have a few possessions. Travel the world if you like. Get married if that suits you. Have some children if that is your desire. All of that can be achieved while still adhering to this concept of enough. Here is the big take away: Own money and possessions; don't let them own you.

A chapter like this can sound like I am preaching. That is not my intent. I am trying to open a window into the future for you to see so you can avoid the mistakes many have made before you. The book, *Your Money or Your Life*, by Vicki Robin and Joe Dominguez, does a wonderful job in helping you with this concept. When you reach enough, STOP.

"Be content with what you have; rejoice in the way things are. When you realize there is nothing lacking, the whole world belongs to you."

- Lao Tzu

68

HELPING OTHERS

If you want to find true and meaningful happiness in your life, find ways to help your communities. Helping others will bring you the kind of personal fulfillment that cannot be found elsewhere. Instead of chasing after your desires, reach out and help others.

We do not often hear this message. Why? No one usually benefits financially from you helping others. The clear majority of advertisements say one thing, "It's all about you." That is not a message that will help you make a better life for yourself and the people you love. Stop seeking external validation and start reaching for intrinsic returns.

Intrinsic? What you do is the reward itself. By giving to someone, you benefit internally in ways that are hard to explain. Your soul is fed instead of your wallet. You don't give with the thought of receiving something. That would be seeking an external reward. No, you give because it makes you feel good to do it.

An example of this idea is explained as we look at a parent. Most parents give to their children in many ways all the time without any thought of getting anything back. It warms the heart of the parent even when the child doesn't fully appreciate the gift. This might explain why so many parents say raising a child was the greatest thing they have ever done.

Here is another example that might help to explain the uniqueness of this approach to life. I help people with their finances for free. Some people ask me why I would do such a thing. I tell them my reward is intrinsic. They stare at me like I'm from Mars. Everything doesn't have to be about money.

You wouldn't tell a parent they were crazy for giving to their children without charging them a fee, right? So then, why do people look at me like I am nuts when I help adults with their money at no charge? That was rhetorical. I think we both know why. Parents do it all the time. It's rare to see someone help others with their money at no cost.

Here is the point. *You can do what the hell you want to do with your life!* Don't let others tell you how to live your life. Don't let others tell you how to help. Don't let others dictate to you what is right and what is downright crazy. You figure that out. Live the life that you want to live, not the life that someone else says you should live.

The more you give, the better your life is going to be. That is the truth I have learned. Unlike most of those advertisements that are nothing more than legalized lies, the message I just provided you is reality once you internalize the reward. Just remember, when giving, do not expect something back. Make it unconditional.

Unconditional? There are no strings attached when you choose to help someone or some thing. The intrinsic reward of giving unconditionally is the greatest gift you can give yourself. When you do it with sincerity and no expectations of reciprocation, everyone benefits, and the receiver of the giving can feel comfortable in what you have bestowed upon them.

Can one person change the world? You're damn straight they can. One person cannot only change their life, but they can change their environment when they fully accept what makes them great as a human being. Fully embrace the idea that you are in control of your destiny and before you know it, you will be.

"The best way to find yourself is to lose yourself in the service of others."

- **Mahatma Gandhi**

69

YOU ARE DYING

You are dying and so am I and so is everyone else. You can use death to help you achieve whatever it is you want to accomplish in your life. That's right. By accepting your mortality, you can live a better life. You can focus on the important things and discard the unimportant as you use death to create the life of your dreams.

Death comes with life. It's important to acknowledge it and strive to live a life that is examined and of benefit to others. Examined? Pay close attention to what you are doing at every juncture of your life. The last thing you want to do is become some type of zombie who spends your days zoned out without any true understanding of where you are going.

How does a person avoid being a zombie? Become as self-aware as you possibly can. Step back and look at yourself from afar. Think of yourself sitting on a cloud as you observe your daily habits. Are those habits taking you in the right direction or the wrong direction? To be self-aware is to examine what is happening at this very moment.

Here is a little trick I have learned. Be crazy! That's right. When in doubt, do something that others (and maybe you) think is crazy. Instead of playing it safe and conforming to your environment, go in the opposite direction and do what others think or say you should not do. This simple idea repeated time after time can take you down a pretty incredible path.

Now, don't be crazy just to be crazy. Find out what it is you want to do and then do it even if others think it is crazy. Focus your efforts on doing what you think is the right thing to do in each situation. Walk your own path and not someone else's.

Live the life of your dreams instead of the life that others want you to live. Have the courage to live life on your terms. That will reduce and/or eliminate the regrets you may have when you find yourself laying on your death bed.

You only get one chance at this thing we call life. Before you know it, decades will pass and you will find yourself closer to death. What will you say when you look back on your life? Start asking yourself that question right now so you have good answers when you reach the end.

Visualize the idea of tearing off the shackles that are holding you back. As you do that, you will have the freedom to live life on your terms as you live an existence that is more in line with your true self. Becoming the best version of yourself will make for a great life.

Live life on your terms. You succeeded at times. You failed at other times, but in the end, you did it your way and that is the only path to finding true happiness, stumbling along and learning all the while. Free yourself and be the person you were meant to be. Be YOU.

"It is not the critic who counts; not the man who points out how the strong man stumbles, or where the doer of deeds could have done them better. The credit belongs to the man who is actually in the arena, whose face is marred by dust and sweat and blood; who errs, who comes short again and again, because there is no effort without error and shortcoming; but who does actually strive to do the deeds; who knows great enthusiasm, the great devotions; who spends himself in a worthy cause; at the best knows in the end the triumph of high achievement, and who at the worst, if he fails, at least fails while daring greatly, so that his place shall never be with those cold and timid souls who neither know victory nor defeat."

- **Theodore Roosevelt**

70

THE HERO

Many years ago, in a far-off galaxy, a guy by the name of Joseph Campbell came up with something called, **The Hero's Journey**. There is much we can learn from Joseph Campbell and this idea. Below, you will see a simple explanation of something powerful enough to change your life AND the lives of the people around you. Embrace the unknown!

You are in an **ordinary world** where life is safe, but empty.

The **call to adventure** enters your life, calling you to something new.

You **refuse** at first because you seek the safety of your ordinary life.

You find a **mentor** who prepares you for the future of your dreams.

You start to **believe** in yourself and what you can do.

You **cross the first threshold**, as you take that scary call to the unknown.

You will be **tested** in this new world by your enemies AND your friends.

Setbacks happen. Surviving and thriving, helps you achieve your goals.

You **begin a journey back** to the ordinary, sharing what you have learned.

There is **one final test** that you must pass on your return. It will be hard.

You survive and **bring knowledge to the ordinary world** you left.

The world is waiting for those of you who are ready and willing to take that call to action. Will it be scary to do what others are not doing? Hell, yes! That's why others are not doing it. It takes a belief in yourself and courage to leave the safety of your ordinary world to enter a place full of unknowns and scary "monsters."

You must be willing to challenge your fears to reach your dreams. Here is the good news. Those fears are coming from YOU. YOU can push them aside and see them for what they are, which is nothing more than negative thoughts running through your head, trying to stop you from doing something different with your life.

I have prepared you as best I can to take that call to adventure. Read this book again after reviewing this final chapter. It might help you in overcoming your demons. Yes, we all have demons. We all have that inner voice that says we are not good enough and we are likely to fail. That inner voice is your own creation. Tell it to get lost!

Ultimately, it will be up to you to follow the path that will lead to a life of more meaning and personal fulfillment. The hero's journey can be used as a guide by anyone who is ready and willing to take control of their money and their life. The power lies within YOU. Believe in that powerful idea and believe in your own abilities. It's time to pick up that phone.

Adventure to follow!

"Follow your bliss and the universe will open doors

where there were only walls."

- **Joseph Campbell**

Glossary

1035 exchange: A transfer of money from one insurance policy (includes annuities) to another. This type of exchange can be used when moving money out of high-fee insurance policies and into low-fee insurance policies. Educate yourself carefully regarding any surrender charges.

401(k): A defined contribution plan offered by a corporation to its employees to set aside tax-deferred income for retirement purposes. This type of retirement account is a place where you can grow your money tax-deferred (traditional version) or tax-free (Roth version).

403(b): A retirement plan offered by nonprofit organizations, such as universities and charitable organizations, rather than corporations. It is simply a company retirement plan that goes by a different name. Fees tend to be high compared to other defined contribution plans.

457: A retirement plan offered by some nonprofits, as well as state and local governments. This option is another type of company retirement plan. One big plus with this type of plan is the elimination of the 10% penalty for early withdrawal if you withdraw funds prior to age 59.

Active management: The attempt to uncover securities (stocks and bonds, for example) that the market has misidentified as being under or overvalued. This approach involves outsmarting and outmaneuvering the other smart people in the room. The past has shown us it doesn't work with any degree of consistency (pure chance basically). Avoid it.

Annuity: An investment that is a contract backed by an insurance company. Its main benefit is that it allows your money to compound and grow without taxation until withdrawal. The main drawbacks include high commissions, high fees, and difficulty in extracting your money. The financial industry loves annuities. That is a good reason to question this type of life insurance product. The immediate annuity could be the one exception worth considering.

Asset allocation: The process of dividing up one's securities among broad asset classes (stocks, bonds, and real estate, for example). This mix may include domestic and foreign stocks and bonds. The asset allocation should be identified only after the investor identifies their risk tolerance, time horizon, and specific goals that are unique to their particular situation.

Bond: A loan that investors make to a corporation or government. The investor provides the capital, and the other party promises a specified return. Bonds generally pay a set amount of interest on a regular basis. All bonds have a maturity date when the bond issuer must pay back the bond at full value to the bondholders (the lenders).

Broker: A person who acts as an intermediary for the purchase or sale of investments. Almost all brokers are paid on commission, which creates a conflict of interest with their clients (also known as victims). The more the broker sells, the more money he makes. It is known as churning, and is illegal but difficult to prove in a court of law. Stay away from them.

Capital gain: The profit from selling your stock at a higher price than the price which it was purchased. Example: You bought a mutual fund at $60 per share, and you sell it five years later for $90 per share. Your profit is $30 per share. If your investment is outside of a retirement account, you will pay a capital gains tax on that profit. This tax will not apply (in the year in which you sold the asset) to an investment that is in a retirement plan.

Cash-value life insurance: This type of life insurance policy is highly "recommended" by most life insurance agents. In a cash-value policy, you buy life insurance coverage but also get a savings account to boot. The investment returns will be poor because of the high commissions and high fees that come out in the early years of the policy. Stay away.

Deductible: The portion you pay when you file a claim on an insurance policy. If you have a $1,000 deductible on a home insurance policy and file a claim on your house after a tornado damages it up to $50,000, you will pay $1,000 and the insurance company will pay the remaining $49,000. The higher the deductible, the lower the yearly premium. The lower the deductible, the higher the yearly premium.

Defined benefit plan: A pension that your employer promises you based on time with the company, your earnings, and usually your age. These are going away and being replaced with defined contribution plans. These types of plans are still widely available for state and federal employees. If you have one, count your blessings.

Defined contribution plan: A retirement plan funded primarily by the employee. It may come in the form of a traditional or a Roth version. Names of these types of plans are as follows: 401(k), 403(b), 457(b), and TSP (thrift savings plan). You must feed these accounts monthly and yearly if you want a comfortable retirement.

Diversification: Dividing your money among a variety of investments with different risk/return characteristics to minimize the portfolio risk. Owning an index mutual fund that owns 3,000 individual stocks in multiple sectors of an economy is one example. Owning a stock index mutual fund and a bond index mutual fund is another example.

Dividend: The income paid to investors holding an investment. The dividend is a portion of a company's profits paid to its shareholders on a yearly basis. For assets held outside retirement accounts, dividends are taxable in most cases.

Dollar-cost averaging: A fixed amount of money is invested regularly. When the price of the asset is down, more shares are purchased. When the price of the asset is up, fewer shares are purchased. This forced savings approach can work wonders over time.

Equities: Equities is a term often used to describe stocks. Stocks and equities are the same thing. You may hear equity mentioned in relation to real estate. That is a totally different type of personal asset.

Exchange traded funds (ETFs): Like mutual funds, they can be created to represent virtually any index or asset class. Like stocks (but unlike mutual funds), they trade on a stock exchange throughout the day. They work for long-term, lump-sum investing. They don't work for investors who trade often and/or dollar-cost average money into their investments.

Expense ratio: The operating expenses (fees) of a mutual fund expressed as a percentage of total assets. They cover manager fees, administrative costs, and sometimes marketing costs like 12b-1 fees.

Fee-based financial advisor/planner: This term is used to describe how a licensed salesperson earns his or her money. Fee-based usually means the salesperson works on loads and/or commissions from the investments he or she sells. Avoid fee-based salespeople.

Fee-only financial advisor/planner: This term describes how a professional earns his or her money. It's a pretty simple thing. You and only you pay them. This help is the only type you should seek when in need of assistance.

Fiduciary: The expert sitting across from you has an obligation to act in your best interest instead of his or hers. When seeking financial advice, this person is the kind you should seek out for guidance. Sadly, they are hard to find in the world dominated by fee-based advisors/planners.

Financial plan: This document should cover your financial life as it lays out a blueprint for your future. It should include your investment policy statement, Social Security withdrawal plans, tax reduction approaches, insurance do's and don'ts, and pretty much anything else that has an effect on your future financial situation.

Index mutual fund: A mutual fund designed to mimic the returns of a given market. Examples would include: S&P 500, Wilshire 5000, and the Russell 3000. These types of funds are ultra-cheap, and because of the cost difference, they have consistently beaten managed mutual funds over short and long periods of time. Never pay a load when selecting this option.

Individual retirement account (IRA): A retirement account that you open outside of your place of employment. There are many types: Roth (after tax) and traditional (before tax) are two. Which one you select will vary based on your current and projected tax situation. Most people would be wise to own a Roth IRA based on the tax-free earnings that will take place over many years.

International stock market mutual fund: Pooled stocks within a mutual fund that are invested in stock markets outside of the United States. This type of fund may include developed countries like Germany, Japan, Canada, and France or developing countries like Brazil, India, China, and Russia.

Investment Policy: A written down plan that describes your specific approach to asset allocation as it relates to stocks, bonds, real estate and cash. It belongs in a financial plan and should be monitored and modified over time as you age.

Junk bond: A bond rated below investment grade. These types of bonds are also called high-yield bonds. Many people own junk bonds as they chase yield (interest on your investment). Avoid them.

Keogh plan: A tax-deductible retirement plan that is available to self-employed individuals. They are relatively easy to set up at your favorite investment management company, such as Vanguard.

Load mutual fund: A mutual fund sold with a sales charge and paid to the salesperson that initiates the action between the investor and the investment company. A load and a commission are one and the same.

Mutual fund: A portfolio of stocks, bonds, or other assets managed by an investment company. They provide wide diversification that is necessary and prudent for the average investor.

No-load mutual fund: A mutual fund sold without a sales or distribution fee. There is no commission attached to your investment. These are the only type of mutual funds you should own.

Nominal return: Returns that have not been adjusted for inflation. These are the types of returns you will almost always see when reading a newspaper, a magazine, or listening to a presentation on investing.

Opportunity Cost: The cost you incur when placing your money in one place instead of another. Paying off debt at an accelerated rate vs. investing your money in your Roth IRA would be one example.

Passive management: A buy-and-hold investment strategy. The passive management approach includes lower portfolio turnover, lower operating expenses and transactions costs, greater tax efficiency, consistent exposure to risk factors over time, and a long-term perspective.

Real estate investment trust (REIT): A mutual fund that owns stock in shopping centers, apartment buildings, and other commercial real estate. Focus on owning publicly-traded REITs while staying away from Private REITs pushed hard by commission-hungry brokers.

Real return: The nominal return minus the inflation rate. Example: You earn 5 percent on an investment and the inflation rate is running at 3.2 percent. Your real return would be 1.8 percent.

Rebalancing: The process of buying and selling portfolio components so as to maintain a target asset allocation. This move involves selling your winners and buying your losers to get your portfolio back to the desired allocations you want based on your particular situation.

Rollover: The term used to describe moving money from one retirement account to another by the owner. It must be complete in 60 days or taxes and penalties will be owed. Usually a check is sent to the owner and it is their responsibility to move that money to a retirement account.

Roth: A retirement plan that places your money into your selected investment accounts after the money has been taxed. There are company retirement Roth accounts (403b, 401k, TSP, and 457) and there are Roth IRAs. Both can be good options, but they are totally different options.

Standard & Poor's 500 Index: An index measuring the performance of 500 large-company US stocks. This index is often cited as "the market." Small and mid-size companies are excluded when this occurs. The Russell 3000 is a better gauge of the entire market.

Stock: Shares of ownership in a publicly-held company. You can invest in stock (also referred to as equities) by purchasing individual shares or by owning a stock mutual fund.

Survivor Benefit: The Social Security benefit due a survivor based on marriage (includes former marriage) or parenthood (includes children that are not your natural children in many cases).

Target date retirement fund: This type of fund allocates your investments within the fund based on the date you select. A 2050 fund will be more aggressive (more stocks) than a 2030 fund (more bonds and cash).

Term life insurance: Inexpensive life insurance that has no cash value. It is pure insurance. It should be purchased when someone relies on your income to live. Annual renewable term and level-term policies that stretch out over many years will work for many.

Thrift Savings Plan (TSP): A defined contribution plan offered by the federal government to its employees (military and civilian). The TSP is the best retirement plan in America primarily because of the amazingly low cost per fund. Count your lucky stars if you have this retirement plan at work.

Universal life insurance: Cash-value life insurance that grew out of whole life insurance. Part investment and part insurance is the pitch, but it is nothing more than a poor way to invest for your future. Stay away.

Variable annuity: A life insurance contract providing future payments to the holder with variable returns based on the investments contained within the annuity. Just another poor life insurance product. Avoid it.

Variable life insurance: A cash-value policy that has part of the account invested in investments like stocks and bonds that will fluctuate over time. The costs are high and the returns are low. Avoid it.

Whole life insurance: Cash-value life insurance that provides level premiums over time. High fees are "baked in" to the product to pay high commissions to the life insurance agents who sell them. Avoid!

Wilshire 5000 total market index: This index mimics the entire US stock market, which includes small, mid, and large capitalization companies. Use this index when identifying a total stock market fund to invest in.

Made in the USA
Monee, IL
04 February 2023